RENEWALS: 691-4574

Coastal Marshes
Ecology and Wildlife Management

WITHDRAWN
UTSA LIBRARIES

Wildlife Habitats

Milton W. Weller, Series Editor

WITHDRAWN
UTSA LIBRARIES

Coastal Marshes

Ecology and Wildlife Management

ROBERT H. CHABRECK

University of Minnesota Press □ Minneapolis

Library
University of Texas
at San Antonio

Copyright © 1988 by the University of Minnesota
All rights reserved. No part of this publication may be
reproduced, stored in a retrieval system, or transmitted, in
any form or by any means, electronic, mechanical, photo-
copying, recording, or otherwise, without the prior written
permission of the publisher.
Published by the University of Minnesota Press
2037 University Avenue Southeast, Minneapolis, MN 55414.
Published simultaneously in Canada
by Fitzhenry & Whiteside Limited, Markham.
Printed in the United States of America.

Library of Congress Cataloging-in-Publication Data

Chabreck, R. H.
  Coastal marshes.

  (Wildlife habitats)
  Bibliography: p.
  Includes index.
  1. Tidemarsh ecology—United States. 2. Tidemarsh
ecology—Gulf Coast (U.S.) 3. Wildlife management—
United States. 4. Wildlife management—Gulf Coast
(U.S.) I. Title. II. Series.
QH104.5.G84C48 1988   574.5'2636   88-1168
ISBN 0-8166-1662-0
ISBN 0-8166-1663-9 (pbk.)

The University of Minnesota
is an equal-opportunity
educator and employer.

Foreword

The understanding of wildlife in relation to its habitat, and the management of these habitats in the interest of hunters, bird watchers and other observers of nature, has evolved slowly from trial-and-error manipulations of poorly understood plant communities to a more sophisticated application of scientific approaches and theories to complex ecosystems. Yet, these methods cannot operate without societal understanding, as many of the decisions on wildlife management have an effect on land-management approaches and hence on diverse resource users. Of still greater importance to wildlife is the fact that land management for various other human activities affects wildlife directly or indirectly.

We have already lost most of the natural grasslands in the Americas and Eurasia, and over half of the freshwater wetlands. There is now international concern for the drastic decline in tropical rain forests. This focus on habitat for wildlife has broadened to an understanding and concern for the role of these plant assemblages in society through their global significance in the biochemistry and diversity of life on the planet. As a result, not only are there efforts to evaluate and save major blocks of natural habitats, we now are involved in restoration and even creation of desired habitats. This involves manipulating the most complex and sensitive of all natural systems, and thus requires thorough understanding of the functions and ongoing processes in each habitat.

Wildlife biologists and managers often have been so involved in developing their science that they have not tried to communicate these issues and activities to the public. But television nature series have demonstrated that public audiences not only can understand fairly complex natural phenomena, but they actively seek films on such subjects. This Wildlife Habitat Series is designed to outline our present understanding of some of these dominant habitats, and to present the conceptual framework, justification, and biological intricacies of management strategies for wildlife while emphasizing the importance of a habitat approach in conservation. Some habitats like tundra and bogs are not actively managed but are seriously influenced by human activities; these also will be considered.

Whether you are interested in understanding these unique habitats or manipulating them to improve their resource values, this volume will introduce you to ecosystems, facts about the way they work, concepts and patterns that guide their management, and conflicts between these habitats and society, as well as needs of wildlife.

Milton W. Weller

Preface

People often visualize the seacoast as an area with broad, sandy beaches, clear blue water, and sunbathers lazily basking on towels or frolicking in the surf. Such scenes are typical of many coastal areas and leave a lasting impression on visitors. However, the coastal region of the United States is a highly diversified environment and, in addition to sandy beaches, contains various features such as rocky shorelines, lagoons, estuaries, and marshes. Of the many features of the coastal region, none receives the public attraction of beaches, but all have special ecological significance and serve useful purposes for society and the wildlife that depends on the areas for survival.

Marshes are transitional zones between the sea and uplands and are a dominant feature of many coastal areas. Coastal marshes are low-lying meadows that are frequently inundated by tidewater from the sea or saturated by floodwater draining from uplands. They contain grasses, sedges, rushes, and similar plants especially adapted for growth in a semiaquatic environment.

The occasional visitor to the seacoast and even local residents often view a coastal marsh as a wet wasteland infested with insects, poisonous snakes, and foul odors. Developers see the marsh as a frontier, an area to conquer and change. Planners of construction projects look to the nearby coastal marshes when considering sites for future development that would receive least local opposition. Marshes are particularly attractive to industrial and residential developers because they contain considerable water frontage, a key factor in site selection.

However, in recent years the public has become increasingly aware of the value of coastal marshes to the local economy and of their importance to fisheries and wildlife.

This book describes the coastal marshes of the United States, their form, functions, ecological relationships, wildlife value, and their management for wildlife. I emphasize marshes of the northern coast of the Gulf of Mexico because this area contains the greatest acreage of marsh and it is the region I know best.

Robert H. Chabreck

Acknowledgments

During the past 30 years, I have been employed by the Louisiana State University Agricultural Center, Louisiana Department of Wildlife and Fisheries, and U.S. Fish and Wildlife Service in research and management of coastal marshes. I have also worked as a consultant in wetland ecology with many other public and private organizations. I am very grateful that my employers have afforded me the opportunity to visit and work in all coastal regions of the United States.

Many people have contributed to my understanding and appreciation of coastal marshes and the living resources the marshes sustain. Individuals most helpful include Clair A. Brown, Allan B. Ensminger, Leslie L. Glasgow, Greg Linscombe, George H. Lowery, Jr., John J. Lynch, John D. Newsom, Ted O'Neil, A. W. Palmisano, Johnnie W. Tarver, and Richard K. Yancey.

My most treasured memories of coastal marshes are those of my early youth when my father, John J. Chabreck, Sr., a duck hunter and trapper, brought me along on his many excursions into the marshes along the northern shore of Lake Pontchartrain near our home.

Table of Contents

Coastal Marshes
Ecology and Wildlife Management

CHAPTER 1
Distribution
of Coastal Marshes

Regional Variation

Topography and other physical features of a region influence the amount of marshland along the coastline. Regions bordered by a broad, flat coastal plain and a gently sloping continental shelf offshore contain the greatest expanse of coastal marshes. Marshes form along the shoreline when sediment deposited by rivers or the sea fill the shallow waters, then extend seaward as shoals that accrete from the water bottom to elevations suitable for plant growth (Coleman 1966). Coastlines bordered by mountainous terraine usually contain deep water near shore and produce conditions unfavorable for marsh development (Seliskar and Galliger 1983). In such regions the adjacent band of continental shelf is narrow and steep, thus curtailing the sediment accumulation and accretion necessary for marshes to form. Marshes in such areas occur mainly along the fringes of river, inlets, or other embayments.

Coastal marshes occupy an area of 9,440 square miles in the United States outside Alaska, Hawaii, and the Great Lakes region (Alexander et al. 1986). Most of this marshland is along the shoreline of the Gulf of Mexico and the South Atlantic and is associated with the extensive coastal plains bordering these regions (Fig. 1). Much of the New England and Pacific coasts have rocky coastlines and contain marshland only in protected embayments.

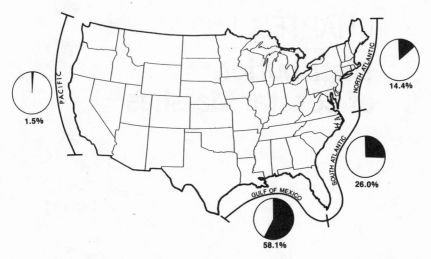

Figure 1. *Regional distribution of coastal marshes in the United States (Alexander et al. 1986).*

Gulf Coast

The coastal region of the Gulf of Mexico contains 5,480 square miles of marsh (Alexander et al. 1986). Much of this marshland (3,800 square miles) occurs in Louisiana and was formed largely as deltaic deposits of the Mississippi River (West 1977). Marshes border the entire coastline of Louisiana and extend inland for distances up to 50 miles. Because of the tremendous width of these marshes, environmental conditions vary and waters range from highly saline to fresh. Also present are broad transitional zones of brackish and intermediate marsh (O'Neil 1949, Chabreck 1972).

Texas contains 740 square miles of marshland in a narrow band along its coastline (Alexander et al. 1986). The greatest expanse of marsh is located east of Galveston Bay and represents a westward continuation of marshes produced by Mississippi River deposits. Marsh of the region displays the gradual transition from saline to fresh and provides wide habitat diversity. Westward along the Texas coast to the Rio Grande River, small marshes fringe lagoons of very high salinity (Buller 1964, West 1977).

Mississippi, Alabama, and the Gulf Coast of Florida contain 940 square miles of coastal marsh (Alexander et al. 1986). Marsh along the west coast of Mississippi is part of an inactive delta of the Mississippi

River and is now nourished by freshwater and *alluvial* deposits from the Pearl River. Elsewhere along the coasts of Mississippi, Alabama, and northern Florida, marshes are limited to alluvial pockets along the shorelines of protected bays and rivers. The western coast of Florida contains extensive lowlands and large areas of marsh. South of Tampa Bay, however, mangroves dominate coastal lowlands, and marsh occurs only in isolated openings among stands of these trees.

Along the northwestern (Texas) and northeastern (Alabama and Mississippi) segments of the Gulf Coast, the land is 5 to 15 feet above sea level very near the shoreline and limits the areas subject to tidal inundation. Southeastern Texas, Louisiana, and western Florida have broad coastal lowlands near sea level.

Atlantic Coast

The Atlantic coast contains 3,790 square miles of coastal marsh (Alexander et al. 1986). Three-fourths of the marshland is located south of Maryland, mostly in North Carolina, South Carolina, and Georgia (Shaw and Fredline 1954, Reimold 1977). Broad, flat coastal plains slope gently to the shoreline in these states and produce vast lowlands near mean sea level.

The marshes in Virginia and Maryland are largely associated with Chesapeake Bay and tidal creeks and rivers draining into the bay. Delaware and New Jersey contain sizable areas of marsh associated with Delaware Bay. Also, scattered marshes occur as fringes along seashores protected by barrier islands. Marshes in New York lie principally along tidal creeks leading inland into Long Island. Most tidal marshes along the east coast of Florida border large rivers and extend inland for great distances.

Unlike coastal regions of the South Atlantic, much of the New England coastline is rugged with rock outcroppings. Marshes along the coast are relatively small (combined they occupy 215 square miles) and subjected to drastic tidal fluctuation (Nixon and Oviatt 1973). They border tidal creeks, bay shores, and other protected waters.

Pacific Coast

The Pacific Coast has no broad coastal plain. Instead, rugged mountain ranges parallel the shoreline and slope abruptly to the ocean

(Inman and Norstrom 1971). The continental shelf is narrow and steep, thus restricting formation of barrier islands and *spits*. Consequently, coastal marshes have developed only in bays and river mouths.

The Pacific Coast contains only 144 square miles of coastal marsh (Alexander et al. 1986) and much of that is associated with San Francisco Bay. Other significant marshes are associated with Puget Sound, Gray's Harbor, and Willapa Bay in Washington and Tillamook and Coos Bay in Oregon. Marsh at other locations consists mainly of fringe zones along bay shores or in the mouths of rivers with sandbars that minimize wave action (Sanderson and Bellrose 1969).

Types of Marshes

Coastal marshes can be divided into marsh *communities* or types based on water salinity regimes and plant *associations*. All species of marsh plants are adapted for growth under a specific range of water salinity and produce best germination and growth where that range prevails. Studies have identified the desired salinity range of many marsh plants and have established a procedure for identifying prevailing salinity regimes and marsh-types boundaries by the presence or absence of key plant associations (Penfound and Hathaway 1938, Chabreck 1970, 1972).

For broad descriptive purposes, coastal marshes often are listed as salt marsh or fresh marsh, reflecting the presence or absence of a contact with seawater. Seawater is a complex solution of various dissolved salts, dominated by sodium chloride. The salt concentration in seawater is 36 parts per thousand (ppt), which means that 1,000 pounds of seawater contains 36 pounds of salt. During high tides, seawater flows inland through channels and is gradually diluted. The amount of dilution varies with the salt concentration and flood level of inland waters.

Salt marsh is the dominant type of marsh and constitutes almost 70% of the coastal marshes of the United States. That type predominates because of its proximity to the shoreline. Along coasts with only a narrow fringe of marshland, salt marsh may be the only marsh type present. Fresh marsh occurs mainly along coasts with a band of marshland several miles wide where tidal water is diluted as it moves inland.

Some marsh classification systems designate salt and fresh marsh as types representing extreme salinity ranges (greatest and least) and encompassing a broad *ecotone* or transitional zone. In fact, the ecotone may also be divided into two separate marsh types, brackish marsh (moderate salinity or *mesosaline*) and intermediate marsh (low salinity or *oligosaline*) (Penfound and Hathway 1939, O'Neil 1949, Chabreck 1970, Cowardin et al. 1979). Seawater trapped in coastal lagoons or slightly elevated marshes, where high evaporation and low freshwater inputs occur, may contain salt levels much greater than sea strength. Such waters are described as *hypersaline* and contain salt concentrations that few plants can tolerate, such as the Laguna Madre of Texas and Mexico (Hedgepeth 1946).

The inland intrusion of seawater and the seaward movement of freshwater govern the distribution of marsh plants and the boundaries of marsh types; consequently, the four marsh types (salt, brackish, intermediate, and fresh) generally occur in bands paralleling the shoreline. Because of the great width of marshland along the Louisiana coast, all marsh types are well represented (salt, 21%; brackish, 31%; intermediate, 11%; fresh, 31%).

CHAPTER 2
Environmental Influences

Geological Setting

During the Ice Ages, the level of the world's oceans fluctuated drastically with each advance and retreat of giant, polar ice caps. When ice caps were at their greatest size, they included a large amount of the earth's water. This meant less water in the oceans, and sea levels were several hundred feet below present levels. As the ice caps melted, water was returned to the oceans and sea levels slowly increased. The meltwater rushed across the continental land mass to reach the sea and greatly changed the land surface; erosion was severe and fast-flowing rivers cut deep trenches into the earth's crust (Russell 1957).

Researchers have attempted to determine sea level at different time intervals during the historic past. Workers have used radiocarbon dating to age salt-marsh peats from present-day marshes and from relic peat deposits found in borings extending several hundred feet below present sea level. By plotting peats of known age and depth, curves were constructed that proved useful in estimating sea level at different intervals extending thousands of years into the past (Redfield 1972).

Studies of historic positions of sea level disclosed that sea level 36,000 years ago was at the same position it is today (Fig. 2). After that time, polar glaciers began to grow; sea level began a gradual fall that continued at a rate of about 12 inches per century for 15,000 years. Then, the rate of fall accelerated and for the next 5,000 years sea level fell at a rate of 60 inches per century (Emery and Uchupi 1972).

Sea level 15,000 years ago was 450 feet below the present-day level, and one-third of the earth's land surface was covered with ice sheets that were an average of one mile thick (Russell 1957, 1967). Then, climatic conditions drastically changed and the giant polar glaciers began to melt. As the meltwater rushed to the oceans, sea level began to rise at a rapid rate (54 inches/century), which continued for 8,000 years. The rate of rise then declined to 20 inches per century, before sea level stabilized near its present position about 3,000 years ago. The rising sea level often flooded river valleys, caused arms of the sea to extend far inland, and formed vast embayments such as Chesapeake Bay, Delaware Bay, and most bays along the Pacific Coast.

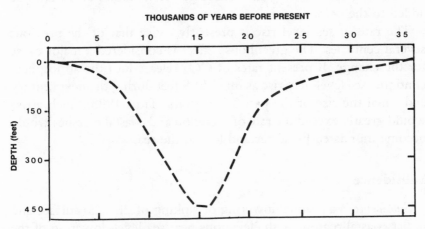

Figure 2. *Sea levels have periodically changed over the past 36,000 years, and 15,000 years ago were 450 feet below present levels (Russell 1957).*

Present coastal marshes developed after sea level stabilized — some appeared soon afterward and others are still developing. Formation of marshes is a rapid process when conditions are favorable. Most marsh plants mature and reproduce in one year and a single plant may produce thousands of new plants from seeds; some species colonize a favorable environment with an extensive system of creeping *rhizomes*.

Although sea levels have been considered stable over the past 3,000 years, radiocarbon dating of peat deposits in marshes developed since that time indicate a continued slow rise at a rate of 4 inches per century (Titus et al. 1984a). In spite of rising sea levels, most coastal marshes have persisted because land-building processes in marshes have equaled or exceeded the rate of sea level rise.

The Greenhouse Effect

Twentieth-century industrial growth has resulted in the release of great amounts of CO_2 into the atmosphere. As CO_2 levels increase, the amount of heat radiating from the earth back into space decreases (Boesch et al. 1983). This has been described as a *greenhouse effect*, and heat trapped by increased atmospheric concentrations of CO_2 is causing a gradual increase in the earth's temperature. Although the global warming is so slight that we do not notice the change, it has increased the rate of glacial melting and caused greater volumes of water to be added to the oceans.

The rate of sea level rise is presently twice that of the previous several centuries. The greenhouse effect is considered a major cause for the change. If present rates of CO_2 release into the atmosphere continue, sea level may rise as much as 9 feet during the next century and equal the rise of the past 3,000 years (Titus 1985). Such a rise would greatly exceed the rate of accretion and coastal marshes would become inundated by water and lost to the sea.

Subsidence

Subsidence is a gradual lowering or sinking of the land surface and in flat coastal regions with elevations near sea level, lowering of the land surface may cause permanent flooding. Subsidence has the same effect as rising sea level, which is caused by increasing the volume of water in oceans. *Apparent sea-level rise* is a term used to describe the combined effects of subsidence and increased water in the oceans, which present a serious threat to the future of existing coastal marshes where both factors are operating (Boesch et al. 1983).

Subsidence is a dominant and highly significant process in coastal marsh that formed where rivers have deposited great amounts of sedimentary material in deltas. Subsidence generally is caused by compaction of sediment below the land surface. The rate of subsidence is affected by the thickness and age of the delta deposit and varies greatly from one area to another within the delta region. Sediment compaction is greatest immediately following deposition and decreases with time (Morgan 1973).

Along the Louisiana coast, firm Pleistocene deposits are near the land surface at the inland reaches of the coastal marshes. Pleistocene deposits then slope sharply downward toward the Gulf of Mexico. Approximately 80 miles southward, at the site of the present Mississippi River delta, the same deposits are as much as 800 feet below sea level. Deposition by the Mississippi River during Recent or Holocene geologic time has formed a seaward-thickening wedge of unconsolidated sediment over the Pleistocene deposits. This wedge of sediment forms the marshes of southeastern Louisiana known as the Deltaic Plain and is a zone of rapid subsidence. The site of the present delta contains the greatest depth of sediments and is the zone of the most recent deposits; consequently, the rate of subsidence is greatest in the active delta region (Morgan 1973).

Although sedimentation is responsible for rapid subsidence in delta marshes, continued sedimentation is essential if marshes are to survive. In zones with rapid subsidence, a reduction in the amount of sediments often causes marshes to gradually sink below the sea. The Mississippi River has changed its course periodically over the past 5,000 years, resulting in abandonment of the delta at the river's mouth and formation of a new delta with each shift. The abandoned deltas were left without adequate sediment for maintenance and gradually deteriorated (Morgan 1973). Chandeleur Sound, Breton Sound, Barataria Bay, and Timbalier Bay are part of former delta marshes that have subsided below the Gulf of Mexico (O'Neil 1949). *Drowned marshes* were the seaward portion of former deltas in the zone of rapid subsidence. When the river flow shifted to a new region, sedimentation and the accumulation of plant remains were not adequate for maintaining the marsh above the water surface.

Even with reduced sedimentation, delta marshes undergoing moderate subsidence may sufficiently *aggradate* (build upward) to equal apparent sea-level rise when the marsh supports vigorous stands of vegetation. Some of the plant remains that fall to the marsh surface become incorporated with sediment to provide additional land-building material. Fresh marshes of abandoned delta systems situated farther inland also were subjected to continued subsidence; however, sedimentation was almost completely eliminated when the river flow shifted to a new course. These marshes have persisted by forming extensive floating mats of vegetation (*flotants*) over the subsiding silts and clays of former river deposits. Today, vast floating marshes persist on a layer of peat and muck as much as 10 to 20 feet above the original deposits (O'Neil 1949, Russell 1942).

Tidal Cycles

Water levels are a major factor affecting plant and animal communities in coastal marshes; a major factor affecting water levels is the tidal cycle. The changes in range and character of tides are influenced primarily by changing positions of the moon in relation to the earth and sun.

The tidal range at any location varies from day to day, month to month, and year to year. The range of tidal fluctuation also varies regionally (Fig. 3). Marshes bordering the Gulf of Mexico are subjected to a daily tidal range of less than 2 feet (Marmer 1954). However, in some areas along the coasts of New England and the Pacific Northwest, tides may fluctuate 12 to 16 feet daily (Hedgpeth and Obrebski 1981, Whitlatch 1982). Tides within a locality may respond in different fashions; south of Cape Cod the range is 3 to 5 feet and north of Cape Cod the range is 10 to 13 feet (Whitlatch 1982).

Highest tide levels occur in coastal marsh during the full moon and new moon. However, factors such as wind direction and intensity, freshwater inflow, and barometric pressure also affect the range and level of individual tides at a locality. The rate of movement and level of tides decrease as water moves inland. The rate of movement decreases because coastal streams become narrower farther inland and carry less water. Moreover, the meandering or winding of streams increases the distance that water must travel to move inland. The rate of flow of tidewater moving across the marsh surface also is reduced by dense vegetation.

Channel size and length determine the rate of water exchange, and interior marshes connected to the sea by large channels are influenced to a greater extent by tides than marshes with small drainage systems (Chabreck 1972). Heavy local rainfall often raises water levels in back bays and other coastal areas with restricted outlets. Tidal effects are thus curtailed until the level of freshwater is lowered to that of the current high tide (Gunter 1967, Nichols 1959). Coastal marshes transected by large, straight canals are exposed to drastic tidal action. In

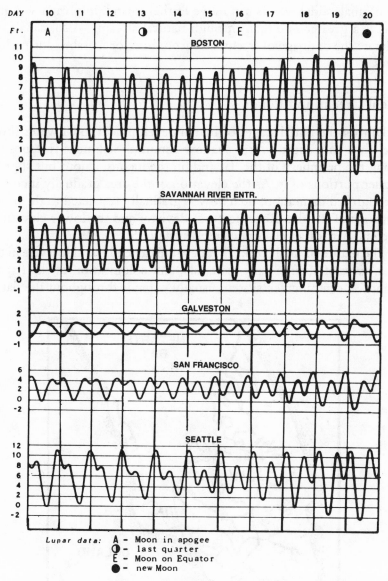

Figure 3. *Variation in tides from day to day and location to location are illustrated by tide curves for selected ports along the Atlantic, Gulf of Mexico, and Pacific coasts of the United States (National Ocean Service 1986a, 1986b.)*

such canals, tidal waters can move farther inland, in greater volume, and at a greater rate than through natural streams. Also, canals accelerate the drainage of freshwater from interior marshes during low tides.

Tidal Creeks and Ponds

During the initial stages of marsh development, tidal water flows and ebbs as a sheet over a shallow mudflat. Sediment is deposited along the periphery of the flat and on the inconspicuous but slightly higher portions of it. As the elevation of the area gradually increases through sedimentation, tidal flow is gradually restricted to the lower portions of the flat. Relief features develop and the lower elevations become part of an elaborate creek system (Steers 1977).

The nature of tidal creeks that develop depends on tide levels in the area, type of sedimentary materials, and colonization of the flat by plants. A central creek system usually extends throughout the flat in

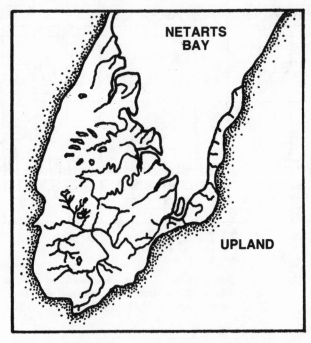

Figure 4. *Stream patterns in the marsh at the head of Netarts Bay, Oregon (Seliskar and Gallagher 1983).*

Salt marshes contain elaborate drainage systems and provide essential nursery habitat for fish and crustaceans. Elevations of the marsh surface vary only a few inches and high tides frequently inundate the area.

the initial development of a salt marsh. In headwaters, falling tides cause rapid surface discharge and meandering secondary streams develop. These flow into large tidal channels with characteristic two-way flow. As the elevation of the marsh increases, it is not flooded by every tide. Discharge is gradually reduced and the two-way flow systems dominate the drainage pattern. Many secondary channels are thus abandoned and form into a network of elongated ponds (Pethick 1974).

Drainage patterns in marsh formed in an enclosed bay are somewhat different from those in marsh formed along an open coast (Fig. 4). The patterns of major and secondary creeks vary with local conditions and time. Tributaries may develop in a *dendritic* (treelike with a major stem and branches), *trellis* (zigzag), or rectangular pattern. The dentritic pattern is typical of marshes formed in embayments (Steers 1977).

Since a marsh surface is almost flat, the boundaries between adjacent drainage systems are difficult to recognize. Anyone attempting to determine the acreage of a marsh drainage system is confronted with this problem. The midpoint between the interior limits of secondary creeks is usually established as the arbitrary boundary.

Soils

Marsh soils contain *mineral* and *organic* components; the amount of each varies with the location and age of the marsh and the environmental conditions prevailing in the area. The mineral component of marsh soil consists of silt and clay particles of a wide range of sizes. They reflect the type of material eroded from the upland watershed and deposited by rivers or washed from the floor of the sea and deposited by waves and tides.

Sediment deposited in shallow coastal waters is derived from several sources and forms the soil or substrate on which marsh plants initially become established and grow. Sediment carried by rivers forms the substrate for many marshes and is deposited when velocities of currents decline to the point that silt and clay particles can no longer be held in suspension. On the other hand, certain Atlantic Coast marshes were formed in estuaries on sediment carried landward from the ocean floor by bottom currents (Meade 1969). Also, marshes of the Chenier Plain of southwestern Louisiana and southeastern Texas developed from Mississippi River sediment discharged into the Gulf of Mexico, then carried westward by Gulf currents and deposited along the shoreline by waves and tides (Gould and McFarlan 1959). *Cheniers* are former beach deposits left stranded in the marsh after the Mississippi River changed its course and began building new marshland seaward from the beach. Some cheniers are now several miles inland from the shoreline and covered with large live oaks, termed *chen* by early French settlers.

The organic component of marsh soil is composed of the remains of plants. The amount of plant material accumulating on the soil surface is influenced by the nature of plant communities, frequency of flooding, and magnitude of tidal currents. As plant remains fall to the marsh surface, they mix with mineral sediment being added from alluvial or marine sources. The ratio of organic matter to sediment determines the nature of marsh soil and varies considerably from one location to another.

Organic soils are classified as peats or mucks based on the stage of decomposition. Peat contains plant parts only partially decomposed, has a brown color, and usually consists of more than 50% organic matter. Muck is usually dark gray or black and well decomposed with none of the plant parts identifiable. The organic content of muck usually ranges from 15 to 50%. Soil with less than 15% organic matter is classified as mineral soil (Dachnowski-Stokes 1940). The depth of organic soil is determined by the amount of subsidence and the vegetative history of the area. Organic layers have been found at depths ranging from a few inches to more than 20 feet (Russell 1942).

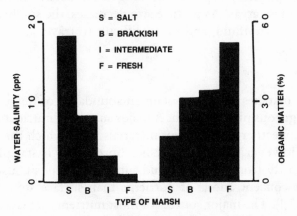

Figure 5. *An inverse relationship exists in coastal marshes between water salinity and the organic-matter content of soils (Chabreck 1970).*

The organic content of coastal marsh soils generally increases with distance inland from the sea (Chabreck 1970), even though plant production may be least in marshes farthest inland (Fig. 5). Exposure of soil to oxygen during low tides facilitates decomposition of organic matter; and, since the range of tides is greatest near the sea, soil exposure and decomposition are also greater. The sweeping action of tides removes some organic matter from the marsh surface and is greatest near the seashore. Much sediment deposited in coastal marshes is carried inland by tidal action and adds a mineral component to the substrate. Sedimentation decreases as the inland movement of tidewater decreases.

Mineral soil of different particle sizes is deposited in different areas of a marsh and reflects the distributional pattern of marsh streams. As water enters a marsh through streams, it overflows the stream banks and spreads over the marsh. As water flows over the banks, its velocity gradually decreases. Larger soil particles are the first to settle out and, as velocities continue to decrease, particles of smaller and smaller size precipitate or settle to the bottom. Deposition of fine particles is enhanced by dense stands of marsh vegetation which function to reduce water velocity and trap the sediment. The finest soil particles are deposited in sections of the marsh farthest from feeder streams.

Low natural levees develop adjacent to streams and are composed of the larger particles. A person walking in the marsh will find the best footing in these areas. As particle size decreases, the soil becomes less consolidated, semifluid, and more difficult to traverse.

Nutrients

Coastal marshes usually contain an abundance of nutrients necessary for vigorous plant growth. A major supply of nutrients in upland soils is the weathering of parent materials from which the soils were formed. However, the vast marshes bordering coastal plains were formed mostly from alluvium, and subsurface deposits usually contain lower concentrations of nutrients than surface soils (Lytle and Driskel 1954). The major sources of most nutrients are rivers and seawater. Rivers transport rich sediment from their drainage basin during flood stages and fertilize downstream marshes. In marshes subject to tides, nutrients from seawater are added during each flood cycle (Phleger 1977).

Nitrogen is a critical element for plant growth and its availability in marsh soil varies seasonally (Brannon 1973). Nitrogen in a gaseous form comprises 80% of the earth's atmosphere, and as it contacts the marsh surface is converted to ammonia by nitrogen-fixing bacteria and blue-green algae (Valiela and Teal 1979). Nitrogen fixation is an important source of the element in most coastal marshes, but greatest amounts are added by tidal waters and runoff water from uplands (Whitney et al. 1981). Nitrogen in the inorganic form is readily available for uptake by plants, but much of the element is often "locked up" as complex organic compounds in plant and animal tissue and is unavailable to growing plants. Nitrogen must be released from organic compounds by bacterial action before the element can be recycled by plants (Valiela and Teal 1979). The nitrogen content of marsh soils does not seem to differ greatly among marsh types (Gosselink 1984).

Seawater is rich in sodium, potassium, and magnesium (Sverdrup et al. 1942), and marshes subjected to greatest tidal action contain the highest concentrations of the elements. Potassium and magnesium are essential plant nutrients and suitable concentrations are necessary for good plant growth. Sodium chloride is the major salt in seawater and contributes to the abundance of sodium ions in salt marsh.

Calcium is also abundant in seawater but generally is higher in fresh marsh than salt marsh (Palmisano 1970). Also an essential plant nutrient, calcium is higher in peat than in muck and clay soils, and much of the element is found in plant residues. Some calcium in marsh soil is contained in shell fragments and is often unavailable to plants. Marshes in coastal regions underlain by limestone generally contain higher levels of calcium.

The amount of phosphorus in marshes is less than other nutrients, is often held in dead plant tissue, and is unavailable to live plants. The element is more abundant in salt marsh than fresh marsh, and fresh marsh in Louisiana with peaty soil is often deficient in the nutrient; an important source of phosphorus is that released by plant decay. In other coastal regions, water draining into marshes from uplands rich in phosphate maintain favorable levels of the element (Whitney et al. 1981).

Sodium is not considered an essential plant nutrient and in high concentrations may displace potassium, magnesium, and calcium from exchange sites on clay and organic particles. The displaced nutrients are then placed in solution and are easily leached from the soil. High concentrations of sodium and magnesium may cause a reduction of calcium uptake by the roots of plants (Richards 1954).

The acidity of coastal marsh soil varies considerably, and studies in Louisiana disclosed a pH range from 3 to 8. Soil acidity and the oxidation–reduction (redox) potential are greatly affected by alternate drying and flooding of marshes and affect the availability of nutrients such as calcium, phosphorus, and iron (Palmisano and Chabreck 1972). Soil acidity is greater in organic soil than mineral soil, and brackish mucks with high levels of sulfate are usually the most acid.

Cat Clays

In certain Atlantic and Gulf coastal regions, brackish marsh soil consisting of noncalcareous, heavy clay may form high acidity when subjected to prolonged drying. The Dutch recognize this condition in soils of acid meadows called *katterklei*, referred to as *cat clays* in this country (Gallagher 1980). In its natural state, the soil is soft and produces dense stands of vegetation. Sulfates from seawater deoxidize and gradually collect in the soil as sulfides. Roots and other remains from dead plants also accumulate in the soft mud and may contain as much as 3 percent sulfur in the form of iron bisulfide (Edleman and Van Staveren 1958).

Under natural conditions, the soil remains wet and the pH is about neutral. However, if the marsh is drained and allowed to remain exposed to atmospheric conditions for several years, oxidation takes place and chemical reactions gradually occur. Iron sulfide is converted to iron sulfate and sulfuric acid, and pH values may decline to 2.5 or lower. Cat clays are thus formed and in such highly acidic conditions plants cannot survive. Iron sulfate may be recognized by its characteristic strawlike yellowish color (Edleman and Van Staveren 1958, Neely 1958).

Early attempts to establish cropland or pastures in marshes subject to cat clay formation have met mostly with failure. Rice was grown successfully in marshes along the South Atlantic because rice requires irrigation during most of the growing season and cat clays were unable to develop. However, other agricultural uses necessitating permanent drying soon met with failure because of the high acidity that developed (Neely 1958).

Restoration of marshland once cat clays form is a costly and time-consuming process. Heavy liming offers only a temporary solution to the problem, and corrective measures require alternate flooding and draining of the land over a period of several years. Management for wildlife is recommended as the best use of marshland subject to formation of cat clay.

CHAPTER 3
Ecological Processes

Primary Production

Green plants are *autotrophic*, producing their own food through the process of *photosynthesis*. With energy from sunlight, these plants are able to transform carbon dioxide, water, and certain minerals into complex compounds such as sugars, amino acids, and organic acids. The food thus produced provides energy for growth and reproduction. The amount of organic matter produced by green plants during a specific time interval is termed *primary production*.

Researchers using clipped–plot techniques have measured primary production and "standing crop" of individual plant species in most coastal regions (U.S. Fish and Wildlife Service 1977). The studies have demonstrated the highly productive capacity of coastal marshes, which is comparable to the most fertile agricultural land (Teal and Teal 1967, Gosselink 1980).

Primary productivity of marsh plants is influenced by a number of factors that vary with time and locality. Temporal variation mostly reflects seasonal effects on production. Seed germination and plant growth are greatly influenced by temperature and greatest production is during warmer months. Temperature influences growth through its effect on metabolic processes such as photosynthesis, respiration, transpiration, and absorption of water and nutrients. Each species is adapted for growth within a specific temperature range. Each has a minimum temperature below which it fails to grow, an optimum temperature at which growth is greatest, and a maximum temperature above which it ceases to grow. Most coastal marsh plants grow and flower at temperatures between 50° and 100°F (Wilson and Loomis 1957).

Some variation in production may reflect broad environmental differences between separate regions of the continent. Again, temperature often is a controlling factor, and production of organic matter is normally greater at southerly latitudes because of the longer growing season. Within a given latitude, several factors operate to increase or decrease primary production. Of paramount importance is the

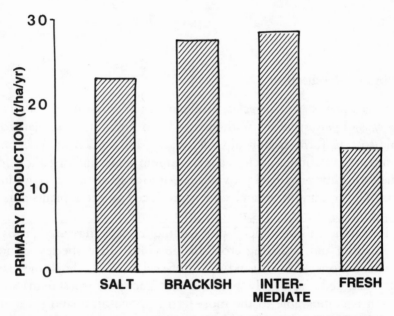

Figure 6. *Estimated primary production of different marsh types in Gulf Coast wetlands* *(Gosselink et al. 1979).*

availability of essential growth nutrients, particularly nitrogen. Other key factors include water depth, salinity, and proximity to tidal streams (Fig. 6). The effects of most of these factors are related and directly or indirectly influence nutrient or water availability to plants (Mendelssohn et al. 1982). Plant density, marsh-pond ratio, and feeding activity of herbivores vary within a locality and also influence primary productivity.

Nutrient Cycling

Coastal marshes exchange nutrients with adjacent water bodies and the amount of nutrients moving in or out of marshes varies seasonally. During the growing season, marsh plants have high nutrient demands and much of the available nutrient supply is bound in living plant tissue. Marshes may import more nutrients than they export at that time. By winter most plants have died, and as decomposition progresses, nutrients are released into the water. The amount of nutrients transported to estuaries by tidal action often exceeds the amount imported during winter (Brannon 1973).

Most research on nutrient cycling in coastal marshes has focused on nitrogen and phosphorus because of their importance to plant growth. The net annual loss or gain of nitrogen and phosphorus from marshes through tidal exchanges with estuaries varies with different coastal systems (Valiela and Teal 1979).

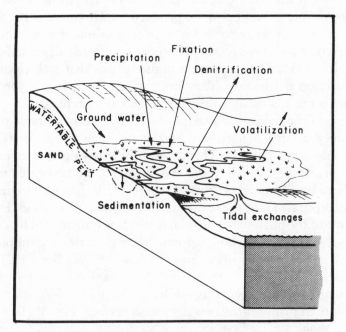

Figure 7. *Nitrogen controls a wide variety of marsh processes, and the amount of available nitrogen and its uptake by plants affects the productivity of coastal marshes. The diagram shows some processes affecting nitrogen availability (Teal 1986).*

Salt marshes act as a transformer of nitrogen, importing oxidized forms and exporting reduced forms, and generally more nitrogen is received by the marshes than is discharged into coastal waters (Fig. 7). Phosphorus also is imported by salt marshes, but they serve as sinks or storage basins for phosphorus received from coastal estuaries and return only small amounts of the element (Nixon 1980).

Tidal freshwater marshes also receive oxidized nitrogen and phosphorus compounds. Most are imported during the spring and summer when plant growth is greatest and exported as reduced forms during fall and winter. The amount exported varies with the accumulation of dead plant material in which the elements are temporarily held. Tidal freshwater marshes are generally net exporters of nitrogen and phosphorus (Odum et al. 1984).

Food Web

Organic matter stored in the tissues of autotrophs in excess of that used by the plants is net primary production. This organic matter provides the basic energy for *heterotrophs* (organisms that are unable to manufacture their own food). Heterotrophs include all animals, fungi, many bacteria, and even certain higher plants that lack chlorophyll and function as parasites. They must utilize food already formed by feeding on plants or on animals that have fed on plants.

Some of the organic matter produced by photosynthetic plants is consumed as live material by herbivores such as muskrats, snow geese, and certain insects. Throughout the growing season, portions of the plants die and fall to the marsh surface. Some of this material is utilized by microbial organisms where it falls, much is decomposed and incorporated into the substrate to form new marshland. However, some of the plant debris in tidal marshes is transported by currents as dissolved organic carbon to downstream estuaries and supplements the *food web* of aquatic organisms (Nixon 1980, Zedler 1982). Some salt marshes have few grazing animals and a major energy pathway is through *detritivores* such as fiddler crabs, which feed on partially decomposed plant remains on the marsh surface (Fig. 8) (Teal 1962).

The *trophic* or feeding structure in coastal marshes, as in most ecosystems, is very complex and involves all living organisms and many individual and interacting food webs. All food webs begin with primary producers, which are utilized as food by *primary consumers* (herbivores). Primary consumers are eaten by *secondary consumers* (carnivores), which constitute a separate trophic level. However, some species, such as the raccoon, may at different times be primary or secondary consumers and are thus classed as *omnivores*.

Figure 8. *Energy flow through a detritivore-based food chain in salt marsh requires decomposition of marsh plants before they are palatable to animals. This extra stage may reduce the amount of energy available to the next tropic level by 10% (Zedler 1982).*

The number of individuals in each trophic level greatly decreases as energy flows from one level to the next beginning with primary producers. Individuals in a trophic level which die and are not consumed by the next higher level are utilized by a separate trophic level of decomposers such as fungi and certain bacteria, which use dead plants and animals and excretia as a food source.

Biodiversity

A community consists of a group of organisms that occupy a particular habitat and often interact. The organisms are attracted to the habitat by environmental conditions that are particularly well suited to meet their needs. The number of species in the community, either plants or animals, is termed the *diversity* or *richness* of the community.

Habitats containing a wide array of environmental conditions also contain a wide variety of plant and animal species. On the other hand, habitats with restricted variation in environmental conditions contain fewer species. Stress placed on coastal marshes by extreme factors such as high water salinity, drastic tidal fluctuations, or low temperature contain few species because of the inability of species to adapt to the harshness (Fig. 9).

A survey of Louisiana coastal marshes disclosed that diversity of plant species decreased as water salinity increased. During the survey,

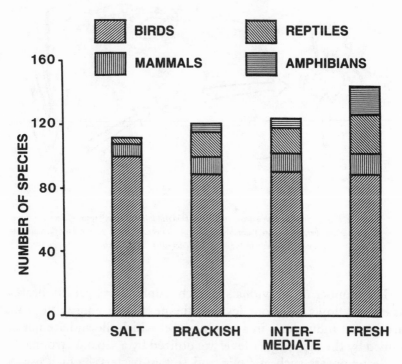

Figure 9. *Richness of most vertebrate species increases as water salinity of the habitat decreases in coastal marshes (Gosselink et al. 1979).*

93 species were encountered in fresh marsh, intermediate marsh had 54 species, brackish marsh had 40 species, and salt marsh contained only 17 species (Chabreck 1970). Most plants adapted for growth in highly saline environments (*halophytes*) also grew in less saline areas. However, most species in fresh marsh are unable to survive highly saline conditions, hence the greater number of species at lower salinities.

CHAPTER 4
Plant Communities

Plant Zonation

The plant species growing in a particular coastal marsh are regulated by prevailing environmental conditions in the area and the availability of *propagules*, such as seeds or roots, of individual species. Major factors affecting growth of plants in coastal marshes are water or soil salinity (Fig. 10) and water depth. Species vary in their tolerance to salt: halophytes are able to grow in marshes where the water salinity approaches sea strength; at the other extreme are *glycophytes*, which require a freshwater environment. Other species have moderate tolerances and grow in marsh where salinity levels are intermediate.

Because seawater is the source of salt in coastal marshes, areas nearest the seashore contain the greatest salinity. Salt content gradually decreases as tidewater moves inland and is diluted by runoff water from uplands. Consequently, plant species with similar salinity tolerances occur in bands paralleling the shoreline. Communities nearest the seashore contain species with greatest tolerance for salt and are the salt-marsh type. Other types consisting of species with decreasing salt tolerance are brackish, intermediate, and fresh. Some species have wide tolerance for salt, will grow under a wide range of conditions, and occur in all marsh types.

Water depth and tidal range also affect the distribution of plant species (Fig. 11). Ponds and creeks that are permanently flooded may support only submerged aquatic plants such as wigeongrass and sago

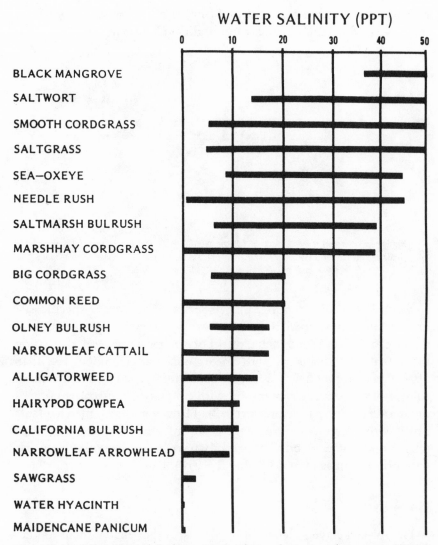

Figure 10. *Marsh plants vary in their tolerance to water salinity and occur in marshes as communities comprised of species with similar tolerances to prevailing salinity regimes (Penfound and Hathaway 1938).*

pondweed. At slightly higher elevations, marsh sites that are regularly flooded by high tides support other species such as smooth cordgrass or Olney bulrush. Marsh sites irregularly flooded by high tides will contain another group of plants, including needle rush and big cordgrass. Because of the small tidal fluctuation along the Gulf Coast, a narrow slope with a range of one foot in elevation may contain as many as four separate plant communities (Chapman 1960).

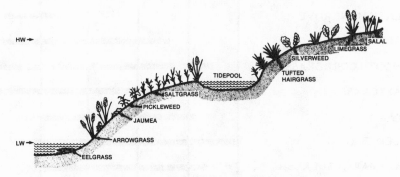

Figure 11. *Zonation of marsh plants in a Pacific Northwest salt marsh in relation to low water (LW) and high water (HW). The lateral extent of the zones depends on the slope and may range from a few yards to hundreds of yards (Seliskar and Gallagher 1983).*

Within a salinity regime, plant species occupying a specific site usually are determined by the nature of the soil. Species such as American bulrush and delta duckpotato grow on soil consisting mainly of silts and clays with an organic-matter content less than 10%. On the other hand, swamp loosestrife, star sedge, and marsh St. Johnswort generally grow on soil with a high organic-matter content greater than 70% (Chabreck 1972). However, most marsh plants grow within a wide range of soil conditions, and organic-matter content or nutrient availability apparently have little effect on species distribution (Palmisano and Chabreck 1972).

Halophytes

Halophytes have specialized mechanisms that enable them to germinate, survive, and grow in highly saline environments. Whenever the salinity of the solution surrounding the roots increases, salinity of the plant tissue also increases. The increase within plant tissue is an adjustment to changes in the *osmotic pressure* of the solution and generally occurs rapidly (Waisel 1972). Glycophytes, on the other hand, are unable to adjust concentrations of tissue salt; when exposed to a saline solution, water is removed from plant tissue through osmosis, and the plant suffers from "physiological drought." Glycophytes growing in

A "salt scald" will kill plants when fresh marsh in inundated during a hurricane with saltwater that remains for several days.

fresh marsh occasionally are flooded with seawater during hurricanes. If the seawater remains for several days, the plants die from a lack of water because they are unable to utilize the water present. Such conditions are described as "salt scalds."

Even halophytes vary in their tolerance to salt. Some species are *obligatory halophytes* and grow only in soils that contain some salt. *Preferential halophytes* produce best growth in saline soils but also will grow in nonsaline soils. *Facultative halophytes* produce best growth under nonsaline conditions but are able to survive and grow in a saline environment. Many halophytes can be grouped into the latter category and grow in salt marsh, because only in this environment can they survive the competition from more dominant species. Facultative halophytes grow more slowly and produce a shorter plant in a saline than in a nonsaline environment.

Halophytes generally have special characteristics that give those growing on highly saline soil uniformity of appearance. Most typical is the development of succulence displayed as thick, fleshy stems and leaves. Other common features are a smooth external surface, small leaves, water-storage hairs, and salt-secreting glands (Chapman 1960). These features enable the plant to control the osmotic pressure caused by the influx of salt and prevent the osmotic pressure from reaching lethal levels.

Plants that develop succulence store surplus water, and salt that enters is diluted in the internal solution. Nonsucculent plants have salt-excreting glands on leaves and stems; after saltwater enters through the roots, excessive salts are discharged through the glands against a pressure gradient by a special pumplike mechanism. By discharging salt, the plant maintains a safe osmotic pressure and retains water necessary for survival and growth.

Plant Competition

Although marsh plants display wide tolerance levels to salt concentrations, seeds of practically all species germinate best at low salinity. In fact, studies have shown that even most halophytes germinate best in distilled water (Palmisano 1971). This raises the question of why there is a zonation of marsh plants into groups of species with similar salinity tolerances. Why are the halophytes not found in fresh marshes? They should be able to grow in a freshwater environment if the seeds germinate best there. Obviously, factors other than salinity also regulate their ability to survive and grow in a particular area.

Of paramount importance is the ability of the species to withstand competition. Competition may be for root space, light, or other factors. Certain species are dominant over all others. Some species are subdominant and can outcompete all but the dominant forms. The "lowest" group are the suppressed species, which are soon eliminated from a site. The process by which certain plant species replace other species is termed plant *succession*. The results are a plant community consisting of species best able to grow under prevailing environmental conditions and to survive the struggle with competing species for the site. Competition takes place not only between individual plants of two or more species but also between individual plants within a species (Mason 1957).

Plant Succession

Plant succession, the replacement of one plant community by another, is an important process in the development of coastal marshes. On river deltas, bay bottoms are slowly filled with sediment deposited during flood stages. As the bottom approaches the water surface, submerged aquatic plants such as hornwort or fanwort are first to colonize the new land. As sedimentation progresses, the bottom is eventually exposed to the atmosphere and conditions become favorable for other plant species to grow. Emergent plants such as delta duckpotato and cattail gradually replace the submerged aquatics and new communities are established. As time progresses, environmental conditions change and make way for invasion by other species. California bulrush and common reed may replace early emergents and eventually woody plants such as black willow may dominate the site.

New land often develops as barrier islands and sand spits when sea cliffs erode and sand carried by currents is deposited along the seaward rim of embayments. The inland portion of the new land is exposed during low tide and often colonized initially by smooth cordgrass. The species spreads rapidly and forms a broad *monotypic* community. However, other species eventually encroach into the community, and as the marsh elevation increases from further deposition, other species such as marshhay cordgrass, saltgrass, and needle rush may gradually invade the area. The successional process thus continues until conditions stabilize and the plant community best adapted to the site becomes established. Coastal marshes are dynamic, and long-term stability is unlikely; nevertheless, some plant communities may persist at particular sites for centuries (Redfield 1972).

Disturbances often take place that cause a "setback" in plant succession and result in changes in plant communities. Brackish marsh along the Gulf Coast that remains undisturbed for perhaps a decade will contain plant communities dominated by marshhay cordgrass. A major disturbance such as fire often hinders succession and permits a rapidly growing species, Olney bulrush, to dominate the burned area. Olney bulrush normally is subdominant and, if the area is undisturbed for several years, marshhay cordgrass will gradually replace Olney bulrush. Properly timed, periodic burning, however, will maintain Olney bulrush as the dominant species.

Other types of disturbance may cause plant succession to further

Olney bulrush, a preferred food of muskrats and snow geese, produces healthy stands in brackish marsh when water depth and salinity are favorable and stands are burned during the fall to control competing species.

retrogress. Muskrats thrive in Olney bulrush marsh and reach greatest densities when a marsh is at that successional stage. Because they consume vegetation and use it for building lodges, muskrats can be a major disturbance. The animals often reach a critical density and effectively utilize all vegetation in the marsh. An *eatout* results and the muskrats either move to new areas or die. The marsh is left unvegetated, and the succession process begins anew (O'Neil 1949).

Low-growing plants such as dwarf spikerush and waterhyssop are usually first to reinvade the exposed, bare soil. After several months, Olney bulrush begins to reappear and, by the end of the first growing season, dense patches of the plant are scattered about the marsh. Throughout the next growing season, the patches become larger and eliminate the low-growing plants as the stands of Olney bulrush expand. After the third year, Olney bulrush once again may occupy much of the area, and scattered marshhay cordgrass usually appears. In subsequent years, marshhay cordgrass progressively expands as stands thicken and eliminate Olney bulrush. After perhaps a decade with no further disturbances, marshhay cordgrass will dominate the marsh and Olney bulrush will be practically eliminated.

Grasses, Sedges, and Rushes

Grasses, sedges, and rushes are closely related families of plants that are major components of the flora of coastal marshes. All are *monocotyledons*, a class of flowering plants containing individuals that produce a single cotyledon or seed leaf during germination. Studies of the Louisiana coast disclosed that some member of the grass family was the dominant vegetation in all marsh types. Smooth cordgrass was most abundant in salt marsh and another grass, saltgrass, ranked second. In brackish marsh, marshhay cordgrass was the major species and saltgrass also ranked second. Marshhay cordgrass was likewise dominant in intermediate marsh with another grass, common reed, ranking second. In fresh marsh, maidencane panicum was the major species. Other common grasses in coastal marshes are wild millet, sprangletop, and paspalum.

Sedges are the second-ranking plant family and major groups are the spikerushes, bulrushes, and flatsedges. The major representative of the rush family is needle rush.

The common names of plants are deceiving and do not always indicate the proper grouping of plants. As indicated earlier, spikerushes and bulrushes are actually sedges and not rushes. Sawgrass, the famous plant of the Florida Everglades, is actually a sedge and not a grass as the name implies.

Broad-Leaved Plants

Individual broad-leaved plants of the class dicotyledons (dicots) are less numerous than the grasslike monocots but contain a greater number of species in coastal marshes. Studies of the two groups, commonly referred to as flowering plants, disclosed that two-thirds of the species present along the Louisiana coast were broad-leaved plants (Chabreck 1972). Broad-leaved plants were particularly abundant in fresh marsh and comprised over 70% of the species of flowering plants. Species of dicots were less numerous in higher salinity marsh,

Sawgrass with its sharp leaf edge creates an almost impenetrable barrier to humans. Dense stands provide excellent cover for minks, raccoons, rails, and many other forms of wildlife but provide poor habitat for waterfowl. The plant once dominated more than 200 square miles of fresh and intermediate marsh in south-western Louisiana but was almost completely eliminated by saltwater intrusion and feeding by nutrias.

yet still comprised over half the species present in the intermediate, brackish, and salt marshes.

Common broad-leaved plants in Louisiana fresh marsh are arrow-heads, alligatorweed, duckweeds, and pennyworts, and various other emergent and floating plants. Narrow-leaved arrowhead and al-ligatorweed also are common in intermediate marsh, along with coastal waterhyssop, hairypod cowpea, and fleabane. Major dicots in brackish marsh include the three latter species of intermediate marsh plus the submerged aquatic plant wigeongrass. Broad-leaved plants are rare at lower sites in salt marsh but, in well-drained areas, salt-wort, glasswort, and sea-oxeye are common inhabitants.

Aquatic Plants

Aquatic plants are able to begin growth and complete their life cycle only in water (Correll and Correll 1972). Woody or herbaceous plants capable of growth in a marshy environment as well as in water are not considered true aquatic plants. Various growth forms are displayed by the group. Some species grow entirely submersed; others may have only the flowers or a few leaves on the surface. Some may emerge above the water as they reach maturity and others may float freely about on the water surface. In some species, individual plants may have leaves underwater, floating, and above water with shapes so different that it is difficult to believe they are all parts of the same plant (Hotchkiss 1967).

Aquatic plants have specific habitat requirements that tend to restrict their distribution. Habitat factors that often limit species to particular localities are temperature and depth of water, physical properties of the bottom, water salinity and transparency, and competition of other plants (Muenscher 1964).

Some of the factors that restrict aquatic plant growth are often interactive. For example, water depth alone may not limit the presence of aquatic plants. Sunlight is essential for photosynthesis; as water depth increases, the amount of light reaching the bottom decreases. Light penetration is greatly influenced by transparency of the water; transparency varies with the amount of suspended sediments, organic stains, nutrients, or other material in the water that increases *turbidity*.

Water transparency and salinity are major factors affecting distribution of aquatic plants in water bodies within coastal marshes. Individual species are able to grow under a specific range of water salinity and occur only where the salinity is favorable. Therefore, in a particular locality, water salinity influences which species are likely to occur. Within the locality, water transparency often influences where the species will occur.

The number of species of aquatic plants increases as water salinity decreases. In water bodies associated with coastal marshes in Louisiana, no aquatic plants were found at sample stations in salt marsh. In other marsh types, the number of species observed were: brackish marsh, 3; intermediate marsh, 6; and fresh marsh, 19. Dominant plants in each marsh type were Eurasian watermilfoil (fresh marsh),

Dense stands of submersed aquatic plants are produced in marsh ponds when the water is clear and sunlight is able to penetrate to the bottom. The plants harbor abundant populations of invertebrates and provide a year-round food supply for native wildlife and winter food for migratory birds.

dwarf spikerush (intermediate marsh), and wigeongrass (brackish marsh). Other major species in intermediate marsh were slender pondweed and southern naiad. Common species in fresh marsh were duckweed, hornwort, watershield, bladderwort, fragrant waterlily, and fanwort (Chabreck 1971).

Exotic Plants

Native plants in coastal marshes have evolved through the geologic past as marshes developed, shifted position, or disappeared. Plant species best suited to local climatic, *edaphic* (soils), and hydrologic conditions became established in a particular area.

Exotic plants (plants of foreign origin) have been introduced and established in many coastal marshes. In many instances the new plants produce vigorous growth and spread rapidly. After a period of years they dominate vast areas in marshes previously occupied by native species. Exotics often are able to spread rapidly because the new habitat is free of insects and diseases that form natural controls in their native land.

Common exotic plants along the Gulf Coast are water hyacinth, alligatorweed, and elephantsear. Eurasian watermilfoil and hydrilla are abundant along the Gulf and Atlantic coasts. Waterchestnut, another exotic species, is common in the Northeast. Many other species occur in all regions but are less common.

The method of introduction is unknown for many species; however, water hyacinth was introduced as an ornamental because of its colorful flowers. Many species were transported across the oceans as ballast in the bilges of early sailing vessels (Lloyd and Tracy 1901). Before venturing onto the high seas, the boats were often loaded with plants growing along the shoreline of foreign harbors to provide stability. Marsh and aquatic plants contain an abundance of water and provided the necessary weight for ballast. Moreover, they were readily available and relatively easy to load and unload. After crossing the ocean, the ships were unable to cross sandbars at river mouths because of the heavy load. The plants were then dumped overboard and the boats proceeded upstream. By this method, many foreign plants were transported and introduced into new areas.

The establishment of exotic plants has produced detrimental effects in coastal marshes. Their rapid spread has reduced stands of native plants in many areas. Also, wildlife species dependent on native plants and unable to utilize the exotic species are affected by the change. Water hyacinth and alligatorweed cover water bodies and eliminate stands of aquatic plants that are important as food for waterfowl.

CHAPTER 5
Animal Communities

Coastal marshes, their associated water bodies, and adjacent beaches and sandbars contain diverse animal life. The abundance of individual species varies regionally and is influenced by prevailing environmental conditions such as salinity regimes, water depth and tidal fluctuation, and vegetational communities. These conditions may greatly differ within a given locality and produce quite different animal communities (Fig. 12). Natural and human-induced changes often produce drastic changes in coastal marshes and the species composition of animal communities using them.

Birds

The vastness and diversity of marshes and estuaries of the Atlantic and Gulf coasts are matched by the variety and numbers of birds that depend on these habitats during all or a portion of their lives (Sprunt 1968). Ninety percent of all bird species of eastern North America have been observed in the Gulf Coast marshes (Lowery and Newman 1954). Forty or more species of waterfowl frequent this seacoast and each has its own set of environmental requirements (Lynch 1968).

Birds are significant herbivores in coastal marshes and help disperse propagules of various marsh plants. They are also major carnivores and play an important role in upper trophic levels of marsh and estuarine food chains (Stout 1984). Birds found in Gulf Coast marshes can be grouped as permanent residents, breeding summer residents,

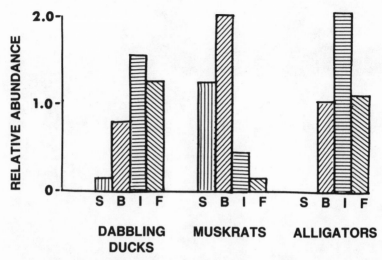

Figure 12. *Relative abundance of dabbling ducks, muskrats, and alligators in salt (S), brackish (B), intermediate (I), and fresh (F) marshes. Habitat quality varies for different forms of wildlife and affects the abundance of wildlife that the habitat produces or attracts (Palmisano 1973, NcNease and Joanen 1978).*

breeding winter residents, nonbreeding winter residents, and transients.

Individual species usually prefer a particular habitat type within a given coastal region but, because of the large number of species and their widely differing habitat requirements, all types of habitats are used. Richness of bird species in salt, brackish, intermediate, and fresh marsh types are very similar along the Louisiana coast. Species richness in salt marsh may be overestimated because most shorebirds and wading birds mainly utilize areas adjacent to the marshes such as seashore beaches and sandbars (Gosselink et al. 1979).

Permanent residents are nonmigratory species that remain in the coastal region year-round and nest, rear young, and winter in the area. Common permanent residents in the Gulf Coast marshes include the clapper rail, mottled duck, seaside sparrow, and common moorhen. Clapper rails and seaside sparrows occur mostly in salt and brackish marshes and are rarely seen elsewhere. The king rail, a close relative of the clapper, also breeds in the coastal marsh but in fresher zones. Unlike the clapper rail, many king rails migrate northward for the breeding season and return in the fall (Lowery 1974a).

Shorebirds congregate along the edge of a mudflat on low tide.

Clapper rails are very abundant in salt marsh but are difficult to locate because of their reluctance to fly. Their body is flattened laterally (from side to side), hence the term "thin as a rail." The compressed body allows the birds to move through dense marsh grass with ease. During low tides, clapper rails may be seen slowly moving along the edge of tidal creeks and ponds feeding on small crabs and snails (Bateman 1965).

Although several species of waterfowl occasionally breed in Gulf Coast marshes, the mottled duck is the only species present in significant numbers. Mottled ducks normally range from the brackish marsh inland to fresher areas. Concentrations also are found in rice fields on the adjacent coastal prairie of southwestern Louisiana and southeastern Texas during summer (McKensie 1985). Preferred nesting habitat is low marsh ridges within 500 feet of water. During dry years mottled ducks often nest in lowlands and basins where the last available pools remain. With heavy rainfall, these areas are the first to flood and nest loss is often high (Rorabaugh and Zwank 1983). However, climatic conditions along the Gulf Coast produce a long nesting season, allow numerous renesting attempts, and increase the chances of producing a brood.

Common moorhens occupy the inland fresh-marsh zone where stands of vegetation are interlaced with ponds and bayous. Favorite feeding sites are along the shoreline where floating plants extend into the water. The birds may nest in marsh vegetation or over water in grasses and sedges that they twist and break to form a secure platform. The young are covered with fine, black down; they are *precocial* and able to leave the nest soon after hatching, accompanied by the parents, and begin feeding on their own (Helm 1982).

Other common permanent residents of Gulf Coast marshes include various wading birds, such as the white-faced ibis, which often nests on brushy islands in dense black mangrove. Several gulls and terns are native species; most notable are laughing gulls, Forster's terns, royal terns, and Caspian terns. They nest on open sandy beaches and bars above high tides (Lowery 1974a). Few shorebirds nest along the Gulf Coast. The most obvious year-round resident is the willet, which nests on exposed ground in marshes and on beaches. It is one of the larger shorebirds and its *pill-will-willet* call draws attention to the bird (Oberholser 1938).

Summer residents of Gulf Coast marshes winter in tropical America and return to the coast in spring to nest. Most reach the Northern Gulf Coast by flying across the Gulf of Mexico. They nest and rear broods in marshes and woody shrubs or on beaches and bars above high tides. Common birds in this group are the green-backed heron and purple gallinule.

The green-backed heron inhabits the shores of lagoons, ponds, and bayous of the coastal region. Its call is the familiar *cop-cop* a name by which many Louisiana residents identify the species. It is less gregarious than most other herons and nests in low shrubs, often over water on a flimsy structure of sticks with a slight depression for its eggs (Oberholser 1938). Local folklore is that alligators cruise the shoreline after young birds hatch, slap the trees with their tails, and promptly retrieve young herons that fall into the water.

Purple gallinules resemble their close relatives, common moorhens and coots, but are more brightly colored. They nest in fresh marsh in close association with common moorhens. Their nests are constructed beneath a canopy of grasses and sedges that they bend over to provide concealment (Helm 1982). Unlike common moorhens, they migrate in early fall and do not return to the Gulf Coast until spring.

Many other wading birds, gulls, and terns are migrants that nest along the Gulf and Atlantic Coasts. However, many species contain some individuals that migrate and other individuals that remain as permanent residents.

The southern bald eagle is the only migrant that nests in the Gulf coastal region during winter. A favorite nesting habitat is dense swamp adjacent to freshwater marsh. The birds build a massive nest of sticks in the top of the tallest tree in the area, often a bald cypress. Eaglets are hatched in December and the parents spend much time foraging in the surrounding area to provide for themselves and the young. Their preferred hunting ground is marshland where visibility is best and prey is abundant (Shealy and Zwank 1981). The young grow rapidly and by March are able to make short flights away from the nest. The eagles migrate northward in April and do not return until October. The adults return to the same area and use the same nest every year (Broley 1947, Lowery 1974a).

Gulf Coast marshes provide habitat for numerous winter residents that breed in northern areas. Some species, such as the snow goose, nest as far away as the coastal tundra along the Arctic Ocean. In addition to the snow goose, regular winter visitors to the Gulf Coast marshes are the gadwall, common snipe, and northern harrier.

Snow geese, including both the blue and white phases, stage in tremendous numbers south of Hudson Bay after the nesting season. From there they make a nonstop flight of 2,000 miles to the Gulf Coast marshes. Snow geese wintering in Louisiana and Texas show a *cline* or a gradual numerical grading from one color phase to the other along the coastal region. Flocks near Vermilion Bay in southcentral Louisiana are composed of 80% blue-phase birds and 20% white birds. Near Galveston Bay, Texas flocks contain 80% white birds and 20% blue. Near the border between the states, flocks are equally represented by both color phases.

The snow goose is commonly found in brackish marsh but shifts about during winter in response to changing marsh conditions. The birds are attracted to freshly burned marsh because of the unobstructed view, the ease of grubbing for roots and rhizomes, and the abundance of tender sprouts. Many snow geese have abandoned the coastal marshes within the past few decades and now winter exclusively in rice fields, pastures, and other agricultural lands (Lynch 1968).

Gadwalls are attracted to shallow coastal ponds containing dense stands of aquatic plants. They arrive in October and spend much of the first month in brackish ponds feeding on wigeongrass. As the supply diminishes, they disperse to other areas where aquatic plant growth is adequate to meet their needs. Throughout the winter, gadwalls are frequently seen in close association with American wigeons and coots.

The common snipe is one of the most widely distributed North American shorebirds. It inhabits marshes, meadows, and shorelines with low salinity where vegetation is short and sparse. The bird feeds by thrusting its long bill into moist soil to capture earthworms and insect larvae. The snipe's rapid and erratic flight has made it a favorite target of hunters.

The northern harrier is one of the most conspicuous birds of the coastal region because of its large size and the slow cruises that it takes above the marsh at low altitude in search of food. Its diet consists of small mammals, frogs, snakes, and birds. Coots are frequently prey because they congregate on large, shallow ponds and are weak fliers. Northern harriers begin arriving along the Gulf Coast in September and many remain until May before they begin their northward journey (Lowery 1974a).

Many birds are transients and make brief stopovers in Gulf Coast marshes enroute to traditional wintering areas to the south or breeding areas to the north. Some species may remain in the marshes for as long as one month; others may remain for only a few days before continuing on their journey. Some individuals may not follow the normal schedule, and when a transient bird is observed during December or July in Louisiana, it is difficult to determine whether the bird is an early or late migrant. Songbirds, shorebirds, and waterfowl dominate this group and typical species are the blue-winged teal, cliff swallow, ruddy turnstone, greater yellowlegs, and yellow-rumped warbler.

Migrant blue-winged teals from northern breeding areas make their first appearance along the Gulf Coast in mid-August. They arrive and depart in waves, making it difficult for waterfowl managers to estimate the number of birds using the region. The first to arrive are adult males; the females remain behind to complete brood-rearing duties and the postbreeding molt. Most adult females and young bluewings do not arrive until early October, after the fall teal-hunting season. By December most have departed, but the northward migration may begin in January and transients again appear in the marshes and shallow ponds along the Gulf Coast. Departure from the state begins in March, but as in fall migration, the birds arrive and depart in waves and by mid-May most are gone.

Reptiles and Amphibians

Many reptiles and amphibians require wetlands as a part of their life cycle, and coastal marshes provide essential habitat in most areas. The number of species in the Louisiana coastal marshes is inversely proportional to water salinity, a major source of stress. Twenty-four species of reptiles are found in fresh marsh; intermediate and brackish marsh each support 16 species, but only 4 species regularly occur in salt marsh. Fresh marsh contains 16 species of amphibians; intermediate, 6 species; brackish, 5 species. No amphibians utilize salt marsh in Louisiana (Gosselink et al. 1979); however, three reptile species and one amphibian occur in southern California salt marsh (Zedler 1982). Amphibians have highly permeable skin and lack mechanisms for combating the drying effect produced by the high osmotic pressures of saltwater (Gosselink et al. 1979). The Pacific treefrog inhabits stands of glasswort in high-salt marsh but is most common elsewhere in freshwater where suitable breeding habitat is provided (Zedler 1982).

Reptiles found in Louisiana salt marsh are the diamondback terrapin, Mobile cooter (a turtle), Gulf salt marsh snake, and American alligator. The diamondback terrapin inhabits sheltered, salt and brackish coastal waters from Cape Cod southward along the Atlantic Coast then westward along the Gulf Coast into Mexico. Individuals from different segments of the coastal plains show considerable variation and 7 subspecies are recognized (Conant 1975).

The Gulf salt marsh snake is abundant in salt and brackish marshes but rarely enters freshwater. Two close relatives, mangrove water snake and Atlantic salt marsh snake, occupy brackish and saline coastal habitats in Florida (Conant 1975).

Although the Mobile cooter and the alligator occur in saltwater environments, the species are more abundant in fresher water. Alligators rarely breed in areas where water salinities exceed 10 ppt (Chabreck

1965). Individuals encountered in salt marsh usually are adult animals that move seaward during high water on rivers or animals displaced by hurricanes. The Suwannee cooter, a turtle of the Florida east coast with habitat requirements similar to those of the Mobile cooter, has been captured far out in the Gulf of Mexico with its shell crusted with barnacles (Conant 1975).

The female alligator constructs a mound of vegetation, termed the nest, usually near a small body of water (Chabreck 1965). In late June she forms a small chamber in the mound, deposits about 40 eggs, then reforms the mound around them (Joanen 1969). She waits nearby during the 9 weeks required for incubation. At hatching time, the young emit a chorus of grunts within the nest. The mother responds to the calls and with her mouth carefully opens the nest, permitting the young to escape and make their way to the den she has established nearby (Chabreck 1965).

Newly constructed alligator nests in coastal marshes are very conspicuous when viewed from the air, and aerial counts of nests are used to determine the density of alligators. Data on sex and age composition of animals in an area are combined with the number of nests to compute the total population (Chabreck 1966). Population studies have revealed that alligator densities are greatest in intermediate marsh and are twice those of fresh and brackish marsh (McNeese and Joanen 1978). Greater densities in intermediate marsh possibly result from less predation on young and more stable water levels (Nichols et al. 1976) than found in fresh marsh and a lower salt content of waters than in brackish marsh.

Fresh marsh supports a wide array of reptiles and amphibians including various species of snakes, turtles, lizards, frogs, and salamanders. Many reptiles inhabit elevated sites, including natural levees and spoil deposits (dredged mounds of soil), rather than the marsh. Common among the dwellers in fresh marshes are the cottonmouth, snapping turtle, and bullfrog. All are opportunistic feeders and consume almost any animals that they are able to capture and swallow.

Fishes and Crustaceans

The network of tidal creeks, bayous, and ponds in coastal marshes supports a wide assortment of fish and shellfish. Each species is adapt-

A clutch of 42 alligator eggs in a nest of marsh grass. The eggs are about 3 inches long and the faint white bands around their centers indicate that embryonic development has begun.

ed for a particular environmental condition that may vary seasonally or with the developmental stage of the individual (Fig. 13). The distribution of most species is largely determined by water salinity, and each marsh type supports a characteristic association of species. Some species are able to tolerate wide variations in water salinity ranging from freshwater to marine. Others, however, can live and reproduce only in a narrow salinity range, and some forms require different salinity concentrations during their various stages of development (Chapman 1973).

Fresh marshes of coastal regions are coupled hydrologically with rivers and streams draining inland areas. Fish and crustacean populations of the two habitats are similar and show only small seasonal variation in species composition.

Freshwater fishes thrive in marsh ponds, bayous, and canals along the Gulf Coast where water salinity is less than 0.5 ppt (Carver 1965). Common species are the largemouth bass and black crappie, with largemouth bass occupying slightly shallower water with higher salinity. Largemouths are abundant in Louisiana marshes but are generally much smaller than individuals found in Florida marshes. For many years the size difference was thought to be caused by climatic variation, with warmer weather in Florida producing a long growing season. However, when Florida bass were raised in Louisiana waters, they grew faster and larger than the Louisiana natives, suggesting genetic differences.

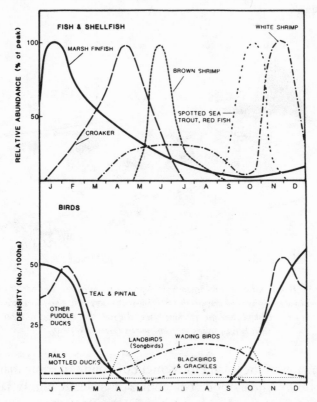

Figure 13. *Species and groups of fish, shellfish, and birds have widely varying patterns of use of coastal marshes and estuaries. Some organisms are year-round residents but many use the habitats only seasonally (Gosselink 1984).*

Crayfish are plentiful in fresh marsh and are an important component of the diet of most carnivores. Alligators, bullfrogs, bass, wading birds, raccoons, and other species depend heavily on this crustacean for subsistence.

Tidal creeks and ponds of brackish and salt marshes serve as nursery areas for many fishes and crustaceans that live as adults in offshore
marine waters (Fig. 14). Atlantic croaker, blue crab, white shrimp,
brown shrimp, and many others spawn offshore and the larvae make
their way to the estuaries. Nursery areas are mostly in the shallow
zone near the shoreline and support high populations of *postlarval* and
juvenile forms. The young rapidly develop in the fertile estuarine
waters, then move seaward as they mature (Gunter 1967, Copeland
et al. 1983).

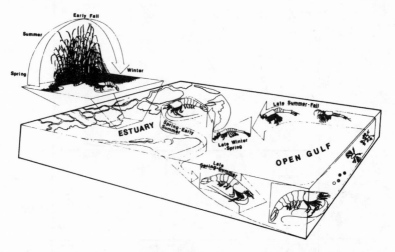

Figure 14. *Brown shrimp spawn offshore and the yonug are carried inland by tides to estuaries
and water bodies within coastal marshes that function as a nursery area. The young shrimp grow
rapidly but return offshore soon after reaching harvestable size, thus affording fishermen only a
short harvest season in inland waters (Gooselink 1980).*

Advantages of the inland movement of young of some marine species is not fully understood. The young can tolerate highly saline water, and nutrients are also abundant offshore. However, some species
such as white shrimp are a prime prey for most larger creatures of the
sea. The movement of young into the shallow bays, tidal creeks, and
ponds of coastal marshes is perhaps an adaptation that has lead them
to a nursery area where there are fewer enemies (Gunter 1967).

Water bodies associated with intermediate or slightly brackish
marsh are a transitional zone, where fishes from freshwaters meet
fishes characteristic of more saline habitat. This has been described as

the tidal freshwater zone of the estuarine region (Odum et al. 1984), and no fish species are restricted to this zone. Instead, the fish community is a complex assortment of species that varies almost weekly. In addition to freshwater forms that are able to tolerate low salinities, the community may contain saltwater forms that seek low salinity during early life stages, transient marine forms, or *anadromous* fishes on spawning runs.

Mammals

Mammals inhabiting coastal marshes can be divided into two groups: those living there by necessity and those occupying the habitat by choice. Species living in coastal marsh by reason of necessity are adapted for survival in a wetland environment and include the muskrat, nutria, river otter, mink, swamp rabbit, and rice rat. Mammals inhabiting coastal marshes as a matter of choice are the raccoon and white-tailed deer. They are equally at home in an upland forest and are adaptable to a wide range of environmental conditions.

The muskrat is the outstanding herbivore of coastal marshes, because of the tremendous numbers present under ideal habitat conditions. Vast areas of prime muskrat habitat occurred along the Louisiana coast during the early part of this century and in some regions the take by trappers averaged 35 animals per acre (Arthur 1931). Muskrat production peaked in the mid-1940s when the annual take in the state exceeded 8 million (Lowery 1974b). Habitat deterioration after that time caused a decline in muskrat populations and annual catches rarely exceeded 1 million.

Greatest muskrat concentrations occur in brackish marsh dominated by Olney bulrush (Fig. 15) (Arthur 1931). This habitat consistently produces the highest populations; however, other vegetative types such as cattails, maidencane panicum, smooth cordgrass, marshhay cordgrass, saltmarsh bulrush, and seashore paspalum occasionally support colonies of the rodents (O'Neil 1949). Colonies rapidly develop in these types when conditions are favorable, remain for 1 or 2 years, then disappear. In Olney bulrush, the animals usually persist as long as stands remain healthy. The relationship between the animal and plant communities is not fully understood, but the environmental conditions that produce vigorous stands of Olney bulrush may be similar to those that produce healthy muskrat populations. The linkage between the two species appears more than the traditional producer–consumer relationship.

Depth of marsh water is a critical factor affecting muskrat populations in coastal marshes. High tides that cover lodges will drown young animals and displace and even kill adults (Kinler 1986). However, severe drought is probably more serious and animals of all ages often die from lack of water while the marsh is dry (O'Neil 1949). Olney bulrush grows best when water levels are within 4 inches of the marsh surface (Ross et al. 1972, Palmisano 1967). Severe drought in brackish marsh causes salt in soil solution to become concentrated at levels lethal to the plant. During such droughts, Olney bulrush is

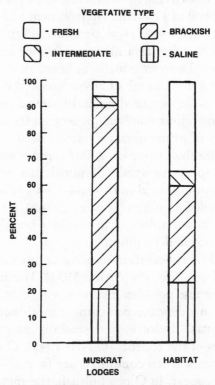

Figure 15. *Brackish marsh produces as much as 70% of the muskrats in some coastal regions, though this habitat may make up less than 40% of the habitat available. Greatest densities occur in brackish marsh containing healthy stands of Olney bulrush (Palmisano 1973).*

Wildlife biologists measure the height of muskrat lodges to evaluate the effects of tidal flooding on muskrat survival. Muskrats construct a network of underground tunnels and enter beneath the lodge into a series of interconnecting chambers.

usually replaced by marshhay cordgrass. The consequences of this condition are usually the disappearance of Olney bulrush and muskrats. Muskrats would be similarly affected in most marsh communities, but the other plant species would not respond to drought in the same manner as Olney bulrush.

Nutrias also are herbivorous rodents but the weight of adults averages 12 pounds, or six times greater than that of muskrats. Nutrias are native only to South America and were brought into the United States with the idea of raising them in captivity for commercial fur production. Twenty pairs were brought to Avery Island in the central Louisiana coastal marshes in 1938, but they reportedly escaped when their cages were overturned during a hurricane. The nutrias thrived in the surrounding marshes and reproduced prolifically (Lowery 1974b). By 1943 they were widespread in the surrounding region, perhaps supplemented by releases of additional animals elsewhere, and over 400 animals were taken by trappers.

The coastal marshes provided ideal habitat and, since natural diseases and parasites were not present in the new environment, the animals rapidly increased and spread across the Gulf Coast. So rapid was the increase that Louisiana trappers harvested over 900,000 nutrias in 1962 and the animal replaced the muskrat as the state's leading fur producer (Lowery 1974b). After the initial population explosion, the density of nutrias declined along the Louisiana coast. Possible causes for the decline were deterioration of habitat conditions, an increase in parasites and diseases, and predation by a rapidly expanding alligator population.

Nutrias inhabit all marsh types but greatest densities are found in fresh marsh (Linscombe and Kinler 1985). They feed on the succulent basal portions of cattail, bulrush, sawgrass, duckweed, alligatorweed, and other *emergent* and aquatic plants found in fresh environments. The nutria is a tropical rodent and temperatures less than 20°F often kill young animals unable to find dense cover. Even adults suffer from cold and their tails may become frostbitten and lost during severe freezes.

River otters and minks are marsh-dwelling carnivores but are often found inland where wetland habitat is available. The river otter is seldom found far from water (Ensminger and Linscombe 1980), except when making overland journeys from one body of water to another. However, mink can live in bottomland forests with a den near water (Lowery 1974b). The river otter is a better swimmer than the mink and travels about in coastal marshes by following waterways. Minks remain mostly in dense cover but feed along shorelines and enter open water only when crossing a body of water is necessary.

River otters reach greatest density in brackish marsh (Linscombe and Kinler 1985). They feed mainly on aquatic organisms; and on low tides in brackish marsh, crabs and fish are stranded in shallow pools and provide easy prey for otters. Minks, on the other hand, are more abundant in fresh marsh and feed on crayfish, rice rats, frogs, and similar forms.

The raccoon occupies a wide range of habitat in coastal marshes. It is an *opportunistic* feeder and consumes both animal and plant materials. Its diet changes frequently as the animal takes whatever is readily available. When crayfish are abundant, it feeds almost entirely on crayfish; when birds are nesting, it feeds on eggs and young birds; when fruit ripens on marsh ridges and spoil banks, it feeds on fruit. The raccoon selects a den in dense vegetation near the food source and remains in the area until the source is depleted or another source becomes more readily available (Fleming 1975).

White-tailed deer survive very well in coastal marshes, but somehow seem out of place in this environment. The species is normally associated with shrub or forest habitats and to see a group of the graceful animals several miles from any trees seems strange. Nevertheless, such sights are common along the Louisiana coast and deer densities there equal or exceed those of most upland habitats. The animals are excellent swimmers and can run at great speeds across floating marshes where a human has difficulty walking.

The marshes of Delta National Wildlife Refuge near the mouth of the Mississippi River was a haven for deer before Hurricane Camille destroyed the herd and most of the habitat in 1969. The refuge provided deer for restocking other areas and crews using airboats and airplanes could capture as many as 25 animals per hour (Smith 1969).

White-tailed deer reach greatest density in fresh and intermediate marshes that contain an abundance of preferred *browse* plants and suitable cover (Self et al. 1974). Levees and spoil deposits provide a retreat when floodwaters cover the marsh. The elevated sites provide good stands of browse plants but during floods deer will also swim out into adjacent marshes to feed (Joanen et al. 1985).

Hair color of mammals in coastal marshes is affected by water salinity of the habitat in which the animals live. Individuals inhabiting salt marsh are considerably lighter in color than others of the same species in fresh marsh. Raccoons and river otters from salt marsh produce a coat that is light brown or tan. Frequent bathing with saltwater coupled with full exposure to sunlight is thought to produce a gradual bleaching of the hair. Fur taken from animals with lighter color has a lower market value than that from darker individuals.

Eatouts

Herbivores are primary consumers and meet their nutritional needs by feeding on plants. Some animals have very specific feeding habits and utilize only certain plant parts—for example, hummingbirds feed on nectar within flowers. Sparrows select seeds produced by marsh plants, and fiddler crabs consume dead parts of plants that fall to the marsh surface. Most species are able to live in the marsh and consume plants growing there without affecting plant growth or species composition. This is the ideal situation, because the consumer can thus be provided a continuous food supply.

Some herbivores, however, occasionally consume plants at a greater rate than the plants can reproduce themselves. Prolonged feeding in one area by such species may eventually result in elimination of plants and destruction of the animal's own habitat. Utilization of plants in an area until all plant growth has been depleted has been termed an *eatout*. Muskrats and snow geese frequently cause eatouts in coastal marshes and the vegetation usually takes several years to recover (Lynch et al. 1947, Smith and Odom 1981). In fact, some eatouts never recover and in certain marshes along the Louisiana coast, ponds and lakes now mark the site of previous muskrat eatouts (O'Neil 1949).

Eatouts occur most commonly in Gulf Coast marshes containing almost pure stands of Olney bulrush. The plant produces a dense underground system of rhizomes, which are the main part consumed. Several years of favorable water levels, free from prolonged drought or excessive flooding, are required for muskrat populations to reach *carrying capacity*, the maximum density that the marsh will support. However, once that point is reached, further population growth usually results in the animal consuming the plant faster than it can grow; hence the eatout.

High muskrat populations hasten marsh destruction, because the animals also use vegetation for lodge construction. Each pair of animals constructs a lodge 2 to 3 feet high and adds new material to the lodge throughout the winter. After an eatout, muskrats in the area either die or move to other areas nearby. Favorable habitat is usually stocked with muskrats also; consequently, an invasion of displaced animals will hasten destruction of that area (O'Neil 1949).

Snow geese are more mobile than muskrats and the consequences of an eatout are less drastic. The geese are attracted to Olney bulrush marsh that has recently burned (Lynch 1941). With all aboveground parts of plants removed, the geese have excellent visibility and can devote more time to feeding and less to caution. Snow geese are *gregarious* and several thousand birds often concentrate in small areas "grubbing out" rhizomes. If undisturbed, the geese frequently remain until the new growth begins to obscure visibility. However, a new burn nearby will often attract the birds and cause them to abandon the original site.

Eatouts by snow geese are generally less severe than those by muskrats. Species such as marshhay cordgrass are not killed by feeding activity of snow geese and revegetation of the marsh is faster. The vegetation not eaten by muskrats is used for lodge construction; consequently, marsh destruction is more complete when muskrats overpopulate a marsh (Lynch et al. 1947). However, studies in North Carolina showed that salt marshes grazed by snow geese may contain less plant cover and belowground production the following year than ungrazed marshes (Smith and Odum 1981).

Nutrias also consume large amounts of vegetation but do not construct lodges or concentrate their feeding in one area long enough to produce an eatout. However, they greatly reduce stand density and in some instances completely eliminate plant species that are preferred foods (Harris and Webert 1965). Species such as sawgrass, cattails, and giant cutgrass were eliminated over large areas by nutrias when the original wave of animals first swept across the Louisiana coast. After the nutria population declined, the plants gradually reappeared.

After a marsh eatout by muskrats, the muskrats either die or abandon the area and the plants are able to make a gradual recovery from the few rhizomes remaining. However, the introduction of nutrias has complicated the recovery process. Nutrias remain in the vicinity and feed in the eatout at night on newly emerging shoots. The feeding by nutrias delays recovery of the vegetation for several years.

CHAPTER 6
Marsh Values and Uses

The band of coastal marshes bordering the seashore is a dynamic and complex ecosystem. It contains a wide variety of plant and animal life and functions to serve humans in a number of ways. In many rural areas, the resources produced by coastal marshes and adjacent estuaries provide a means of livelihood for local inhabitants. Trappers, hunters, and fishermen were the earliest explorers and settlers of this country and the first to recognize the value of the marshes for fish and wildlife. Farmers also made early use of marshes for livestock grazing and hay production. These activities have continued until the present, but today coastal marshes also are important for recreation such as sport fishing and hunting, photography, bird watching, nature studies, and other activities valuable to society.

Sport Hunting

Sport hunting is an outdoor activity enjoyed by millions of Americans. This activity is foremost in coastal marshes because of the large numbers of migratory waterfowl that congregate there during winter. The marshes and adjacent ponds, lakes, lagoons, and bays provide a diversity of habitats that meet the requirements of all species (Lynch 1967). Coastal states that contain an abundance of quality waterfowl habitat outside the coastal zone almost invariably find greatest concentrations of the birds in coastal wetlands.

Chesapeake Bay is the wintering site of an estimated 1.5 million

Most Canada geese that winter in the upper Chesapeake Bay region feed in agricultural fields and roost on shallow esturaine waters. Some birds winter in the coastal marshes, feed on marsh grasses and sedges, and roost on the larger marsh ponds and impoundments (Stewart 1962).

waterfowl, which comprises 35% of all wintering waterfowl from Maine to Florida. The bay contains extensive, varied wetland habitat and waterfowl using this habitat have historically been of keen interest to sportsmen (Perry et al. 1981).

Louisiana contains a variety of waterfowl habitats other than coastal marshes such as swamps, oxbow lakes, reservoirs, and agricultural land (Williams and Chabreck 1985). Coastal marshes make up less than 15% of the total area of the state, yet over 50% of the ducks and geese harvested in the state are taken in the coastal marshes (St. Amant 1959).

Coots, rails, gallinules, and snipe are also game birds taken in coastal marshes. Coots form large rafts on shallow ponds containing dense stands of aquatic plants. Coots are attracted to duck decoys and most birds harvested are taken by duck hunters. Rails and gallinules generally remain in dense cover and since the birds are reluctant to fly, few are taken by hunters. Snipe inhabit high, well-drained marsh where vegetation cover is thin and patchy. When flushed by a hunter, snipe fly very rapidly and in an erratic course, and only the most skilled marksmen are able to bag the elusive birds.

White-tailed deer, swamp rabbits, and marsh rabbits are common game mammals in coastal marshes. Most animals harvested are taken by hunters who live nearby. Rabbits remain in dense cover and are often hunted on low ridges with beagles. To most hunters, the excitement of the chase is a major part of the hunting experience.

Fur Harvests

Farming was a summer activity for the early settlers and fall and winter months often were occupied with hunting and trapping. Trapping provided an excellent means for coastal inhabitants to supplement their incomes. Muskrats were the primary species taken by trappers in Gulf and Atlantic coastal marshes. Revenue generated from the tremendous harvest in Louisiana during the early twentieth century was important to landowners as well as trappers and helped preserve the marshes. In many years the value of the animals harvested in Louisiana exceeded $5 million. Marshlands were generally considered wastelands by most people, and landowners were offered government-sponsored programs to drain the marshes and put them to other uses. However, the great fur harvests with practically no initial investment provided the necessary incentive for most landowners to keep the marshes as wetlands (Arthur 1931).

Trappers initiated the first efforts to manage marshes for the purpose of improving wildlife habitat. They were inspired by the value of muskrats and the realization that maintenance and improvement of habitat quality were necessary to maximize muskrat production (Wilson 1967). Not only did muskrats benefit from the effort but so did other forms of wildlife, such as snow geese. Over the years, harvest of fur resources has continued as an important use of coastal marshes. In addition to muskrats, important furbearers in coastal marshes are raccoons, river otters, minks, and nutrias. States that are consistent leaders in fur production are those with the largest acreages of marshland along their coastlines (Chabreck 1979).

Fisheries Harvests

The coastal zone, including estuaries and the supporting marsh systems, are important producers of fishes and crustaceans. As much as three-fourths of the fish and shellfish harvested in the United States in some years is comprised of estuarine-dependent species. Seven of the ten most commercially important species or species groups nationwide occupy this habitat (Chapman 1973).

The world demand for animal protein is steadily increasing; menhaden, an estuarine-dependent finfish and the leading species in terms of pounds landed, is becoming progressively more important in supplying the protein demand. Menhaden are used mainly as a protein supplement in food of domestic animals (Sykes 1968).

Estuaries and coastal marshes also are of tremendous value for sport fishing. The number of sport fishermen in this country is increasing at a faster rate than the human population and since the greatest concentration of humans is near the coast, the increased demand for recreational fishing places more pressure on coastal waters. In addition to the recreational value of fishing to local residents, communities near the coast benefit from the revenue provided by visiting anglers. Tourism is an important industry in coastal states, and a survey in Florida disclosed that almost one-third of the visitors came to the state to fish (Chapman 1973, Brantly 1980).

Hurricane Protection

Several severe hurricanes usually strike some portion of the Gulf or Atlantic Coast each summer. During 1985 three hurricanes struck the Louisiana coast and caused tremendous damage to barrier islands, marshes, wildlife, and human developments. Hurricanes form over warm waters of the sea and move inland with strong winds and high tides. Wind damage can be quite severe, but the most destructive aspect of hurricanes is high tides, especially when strong currents are present. Tide levels often exceed 6 feet above normal, and during Hurricane Camille in 1969, the rushing water blanketed the marshes of the Mississippi River delta to a depth of 17 feet (Chabreck and Palmisano 1973).

Villages situated near the coast often receive the full force of hurricanes and property losses are usually severe. Municipalities buffered

Tidewaters driven by hurricane force winds occasionally inundate low-lying coastal areas. Rushing currents associated with hurricanes cause extensive losses of wildlife and severely erode marshes.

from the sea by a broad band of marshland are mostly protected from extensive flooding. Barrier islands and other beach deposits are the first line of storm defense (Clark 1974). After these are topped by rising tides, the water surges inland and meets the second line of defense, the coastal marshes (Fig. 16). Marshes provide a drag on the rushing water and its velocity decreases with distance inland (Gosselink 1984). The effectiveness of marshland in reducing the inland advancement of hurricane–driven tides is not only regulated by the width of marshes, but also by the nature of the marsh surface (Ensminger and Nichols 1958). Marshes comprised of dense, unbroken stands of tall vegetation provide the greatest resistance to water flow. Storm waters move farther inland across low coastal regions containing large embayments or that are transected by large, straight canal systems.

Water Quality Improvement

Fresh marshes that lie between the estuarine waters and rivers flowing seaward from upland regions partially filter pollutants, such as nutrients and heavy metals, carried by rivers. Concentrations of the pollutants thus are reduced and water quality improved before the water flows into estuaries (Odum et al. 1984). Unfortunately, most drainage systems flowing to the coast have well-defined channels and the waste products they carry remain largely in the channels. Water moves across marshes only when streams overflow their banks. Salt marshes also remove some pollutants from water, but salt marshes are closer to the sea than fresh marshes and contaminated water may enter estuaries before subsequent tides can move it over salt marshes (Craig et al. 1979).

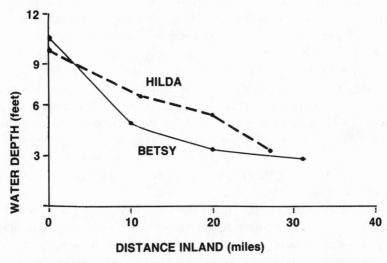

Figure 16. *Reduction in the depth of flooding as hurricanes Hilda and Betsy swept inland across coastal marshes in Louisiana.*

A considerable number of fresh marshes are used for *tertiary* treatment of sewage effluents (Valiela et al. 1976). However, as municipalities along the coast continue to grow, additional marshes will be incorporated into waste-treatment programs. The limits of marshes to function as waste-removal systems, whether marshes would eventually become saturated with pollutants, are not known. The absorptive capacity varies from one marsh area to another; nevertheless, marshes are much more effective at removing pollutants than are estuaries and other coastal waters (Valiela et al. 1976). In spite of the cleansing capacity of marshes, uptake of heavy metals and other toxic materials by plants eventually may result in contamination of wildlife food supplies with accelerated use of coastal marshes as waste-removal systems (OTA 1984).

Livestock Grazing

Portions of the Gulf Coast marshes were under grazing pressure from large herds of bisons long before the first Europeans arrived on the North American continent. Although the animals are normally portrayed as inhabitants of western plains, they actually ranged throughout most of the eastern United States and occurred along the Gulf Coast to northern Florida (Lowery 1974b). Bayou Terre aux Boeufs, a portion of a former Mississippi River delta, was so named by early French explorers because bison spent the winter months there (Arthur 1931). However, the best range for the large grazers was the firm coastal marshes of Texas and southwestern Louisiana.

The first settlements in this country were situated near the coast and marshes were used as rangeland and a source of hay for domestic livestock, mainly cattle and horses. In fact, marshhay was so important that the sites selected for placement of many towns along the New England coast were those best suited for producing fresh and salt marshhay (Nixon 1982).

Coastal marshes are no longer used for hay production, but livestock grazing is still a common practice. Most marshes are not suitable for grazing, because the soil is too soft to support the weight of a cow (Neely 1967). However, Atlantic and Gulf Coast marshes that can be grazed provide good range; with moderate stocking, cattle can maintain satisfactory weight on Gulf Coast marshes during most winters without supplemental feeding.

Major problems associated with livestock grazing in coastal marshes are periodic mosquito outbreaks and tidal flooding of grazing areas (Chapman 1960, Reimold 1976). Livestock losses often are quite severe when a coastal region is struck by a major hurricane. To reduce the problems with insects and tidal flooding, many ranchers in Texas and Louisiana use inland pastures during summer and move cattle to seashore marshes only during winter. Some landowners have enclosed marshland with a continuous levee and installed pumps to remove surface water. This practice destroys the area as a wetland environment and often leads to subsidence when *oxidation* causes organic matter in soil to disappear.

Firm coastal marshes are used as cattle range in many areas. The effects of cattle grazing on wildlife varies with the cattle stocking rate, season of the year, and wildlife species involved. Light grazing during spring and summer is often beneficial to wildlife but overgrazing is generally detrimental to wildlife and cattle.

The relationship of cattle grazing to wildlife in coastal marshes varies with the wildlife species involved and the cattle-stocking rate. Overgrazing by cattle is detrimental to practically all wildlife, except common snipe and other shorebirds that require broad, open areas. However, overgrazing is not considered a wise range-management practice and is detrimental to cattle as well as wildlife (Chabreck 1968a).

Summer grazing reduces production of duck food when cattle graze annual grasses whose seeds are important duck foods. However, habitat for snow geese often is improved when moderate grazing reduces dense stands of mature vegetation and causes growth of tender sprouts. Moreover, shorter vegetation in grazed marshes provides feeding geese with better visibility, an important factor attracting the birds to an area (Chabreck 1968a).

When cattle graze muskrat marshes, they trample the underground runs of muskrats and often destroy lodges (O'Neil 1949). Muskrats feed mostly on underground parts of plants; consequently, cattle do not compete directly with muskrats for food. Some competition exists between cattle, snow geese, nutrias, and swamp rabbits for food, but destruction of denning cover by cattle grazing has a greater impact on the wild mammals.

CHAPTER 7
Alteration and Loss of Marshes

The physical and biological processes that create coastal marshes operate very slowly and centuries often are required for a shallow embayment to be filled with sediment and colonized with emergent plants. Studies at Barnstable Marsh in Massachusetts traced the developmental process of the marsh and disclosed that over 3,000 years were required for it to reach its present size (Redfield 1967). Deltaic marshes formed from sediment deposited by the Mississippi River began their development almost 5,000 years ago (Kolb and Van Lopik 1958).

The processes that cause alteration or loss of some marshes may occur much more rapidly. During a period of only a few hours, high tides driven by hurricane-force winds may revert thousands of acres of marshland to open water. Hurricanes are only one of the natural processes causing loss of marshes; losses from subsidence and rise in sea level are more gradual but damage may be even more severe. Much marsh loss also is caused by humans and when coupled with that caused by natural processes, results in considerable reduction in the amount of marshland along the coasts.

From 1922 to 1954, marshes along the Atlantic and Gulf coasts were lost at a rate of 0.2% per year; however, between 1954 and 1974 the rate increased to 0.5% per year (Gosselink and Baumann 1980). The rate at which marsh is converted to open water continues to increase, and annual land loss along the southeastern Louisiana coast is now estimated at almost 40 square miles or in excess of 0.8% per year (Gagliano et al. 1981).

Scattered clumps of vegetation mark the location of a formerly productive marshland. Loss of plants on the area was associated primarily with excessive flooding, increased water salinity, and erosion.

Hurricanes

Although coastal marshes help reduce the inland movement of hurricane-driven floodwaters, damage to the marshes is often quite severe. In fact, hurricanes may be the most destructive force causing alteration and loss of coastal marshes and decimation of wildlife populations. If not the most destructive, hurricanes are certainly the most apparent force. Sport fishermen, who frequently traverse the coastal marshes of Louisiana, have problems navigating after major hurricanes. Familiar landmarks are often missing; broad marshes may be reduced to scattered islands, and islands previously present may have disappeared.

Marsh-ecology studies in progress before two major hurricanes struck the Louisiana coast made it possible for researchers to evaluate the effects of hurricanes on marshes and wildlife. Marsh Island Wildlife Refuge along the central Louisiana coast was struck by Hurricane Audrey in June 1957 and the marshes were covered with 7 feet of water pushed by strong winds and currents. Marsh openings were increased 140% and nutria populations were reduced by an estimated 70% (Harris and Chabreck 1958). Portions of the marsh sod (1 foot thick and 3–5 feet in diameter) were displaced by the storm and deposited in water bodies, thus restricting boat access on the refuge for several years.

Losses of marshes and wildlife populations were similar at the nearby Rockefeller Wildlife Refuge. The mortality of muskrats, nutrias, raccoons, rabbits, and deer was estimated at 60%. Carcasses of more than 200 birds, mostly rails and gallinules, were observed in piles of debris in one small area. Levees and other water-control structures forming habitat-management units on the refuge were severely damaged by the storm (Ensminger and Nichols 1957).

A study following Hurricane Camille (August 1969) provided data that could be compared with data collected before the hurricane. In general, the size of openings in stands of vegetation increased 118% during the storm. Marshes on firm mineral soil were damaged less severely than those with high contents of organic matter. Several large flotants (floating marshes) covering about 200 acres on Delta National Wildlife Refuge were broken into a network of small floating islands. Several other flotants containing a high nutria population and a large herd of white-tailed deer were completely washed away by the hurricane. Highly productive coastal marshes were reduced to open embayments over a period of several hours (Chabreck and Palmisano 1973).

Rise in Sea Level

Our present coastal marshes were formed during the period of relative stability of the world's oceans that has existed over the past 3,000 years. Stable sea levels allow coastal marshes to become much more extensive than when the oceans are rapidly rising or falling. However, recent increases in the rate of sea level rise present a growing threat to coastal marshes in the foreseeable future (Titus et al. 1984a).

Land subsidence has a similar effect and further adds to the problem of rising sea level in most coastal regions. Rise in sea level is fairly constant worldwide, but subsidence rates vary considerably among areas. Their combined effects (apparent sea level rise) will likely cause extensive marsh loss during the next century, and the amount of loss will vary with the magnitude of sea level rise (Fig. 17). In South Carolina, apparent sea level is predicted to rise from 30 to 57 inches during the next century (Titus 1985). A 35-inch rise in that state would drown an estimated 50% of the coastal marshes and a 50-inch rise would destroy almost 80%. A 36-inch rise in Louisiana would drown almost all the marshes because of the flat nature of the coastal region (Titus et al. 1984b). The rise predicted by Titus for coastal Louisiana is between 44 and 84 inches (Titus 1985) and suggests that coastal marshes there may be lost sooner than in other areas. The excessive rise will be expedited by the rapid subsidence associated with deltaic deposits in that state. Effects of the increase in apparent sea level rise are now very evident along the Louisiana coast and play an important role in the increased marsh loss noted in recent years (Craig et al. 1979, Gagliano et al. 1981).

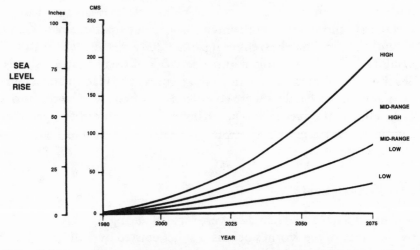

Figure 17. *Estimates of rise in sea level during the next century vary from 20 to 80 inches because of uncertainties regarding factors that are affecting global warming. However, a rise between 36 and 54 inches appears most likely (Hoffman et al. 1983).*

Rise in sea level causes marsh loss through increased erosion and excessive flooding of marsh plants (Fig. 18). Emergent plants are adapted for reproduction and growth under a specific range of water depths and salinities (Chabreck 1982a). When sea level exceeds marsh *aggradation*, water depths eventually exceed the flood-tolerance limits of plants and the plants die. Also, as water depths increase, waves become larger and shoreline erosion magnifies. Barrier islands and beaches protecting marshes from the sea may be destroyed (Titus et al. 1984). Interior saltwater barriers such as natural levees and low ridges may erode or become inundated by the rising waters. Without these barriers, saltwater can move farther inland, thus exposing marsh plants in fresher zones to salinities above their tolerance limits (Chabreck 1981).

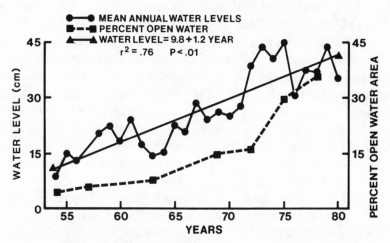

Figure 18. *Marsh loss is reflected by the increase in open water area with time and is strongly related to increased water levels associated with rise in sea depths and subsidence. As water levels rise, shoreline erosion increases in Louisiana and marsh plants are killed by saltwater instrusion and inundation (Baumann and DeLaune 1982).*

Flood Control

Historically, the Mississippi River has sent vast quantities of freshwater and alluvium to the Gulf of Mexico and formed the large band of marshland along the Louisiana coast. During flood stage, the river fanned out through many of its former channels and other streams to reach the Gulf (Morgan 1973). Overbank flooding often carried water and sediment over the marshes as sheet flow and maintained *horizontal zonation* of marsh types. Also, nutrient-rich sediment added to the marsh and associated water bodies enhanced productivity, maintained marsh elevations, and promoted land building.

Because of several disastrous floods, the Mississippi River Commission was formed in 1879 and began levee construction along the river in 1882. Completion of the levee system required many years, but today levees extend southward to the active delta (about 60 miles south of New Orleans) (U.S. Army Corps of Engineers 1976). One-third of the Mississippi River flow is diverted through the Atchafalaya River, which is rapidly building new marshland in a growing delta. However, all other *distributaries* of the Mississippi were sealed by levees; the remainder of its flow is forced down the main channel to the Gulf of Mexico. Sediment carried by the river is now deposited off the edge of the continental shelf in water several hundred feet deep and is lost (Morgan 1973, Titus et al. 1984b).

The absence of river flow through the marshes has hastened salt-water intrusion and eliminated the sediment supply necessary for maintaining marsh elevations. Organic matter deposited by marsh plants was able to offset natural land subsidence for many years and to maintain marsh elevations. However, with increased sea-level rises since 1959, vast marsh areas along the Louisiana coast are becoming inundated (Hatton et al. 1983). When the depth of flooding exceeds the tolerance level of emergent plants, marsh is lost and an open body of water is thus formed.

The damming or diversion of rivers greatly reduces freshwater runoff destined for downstream estuaries and coastal marshes. Also, much sediment carried by a river is retained by a dam. Rivers are dammed to impound water for flood control, water supply, hydro-electric power, navigation, recreation, and other purposes. Reduced river flow produces changes in coastal systems similar to those caused by enclosing a river with levees and in many cases may be more severe. It is a most critical problem facing some of the largest and most important estuaries such as San Francisco Bay and most Texas bays. Freshwater flow to Corpus Christi Bay was reduced by upstream users to a point where the estuary now becomes hypersaline during most summers (Chapman 1973).

Draining and Filling

Marshland reclamation for agriculture began in the eighteenth century and by the mid-nineteenth century, 90% of the United States rice crop was grown in the coastal region of North Carolina, South Carolina, and Georgia. Coastal marshes and swamps were cleared, diked, and drained for the crop. Most owners discontinued farming the area after the Civil War, and soon thereafter severe hurricanes damaged levees, causing remaining owners to abandon operations. Today, however, many of the levees have been repaired and the diked marshes now form management units that provide habitat for migratory waterfowl (Neely 1967).

Similar marsh reclamation was attempted in Louisiana during the early twentieth century. Several large areas with highly organic soil were diked, drained, and used for growing dryland crops. However, most of these failed because of seepage, deterioration of levees, and oxidation of the organic soil. In fact, the marsh level was lowered to such an extent that large rectangular lakes were formed when water reentered the areas (Craig et al. 1979).

Not all marsh-drainage efforts have met with failure, and much coastal marsh with firm mineral soil has been successfully dewatered by leveeing and pumping. These areas are now used for cropland, cattle pasture, residential areas, industrial sites, and many other purposes. In southwestern Louisiana, over 90,000 acres or 15% of the coastal wetlands have been drained for pasture and crops (Chabreck 1972).

The ditching of coastal marshes for mosquito control has been widely practiced on the Atlantic Coast. The ditches, placed in a netlike

Industrial and residential areas have been constructed in coastal areas by draining and filling marshes.

Common reed frequently invades coastal marshes where drainage patterns have been altered by ditching and canal dredging. When dense stands of the robust plant invade a marsh, other species of greater value as wildlife food are eliminated and habitat quality decreases.

pattern, effectively drain or alter hydrological patterns and cause changes in plant communities. Ditching began in 1912 and progressed rapidly as public works projects. By 1938 over one-half million acres or 90% of the tidewater marshes between Maine and Virginia were affected. Studies have shown that ditching greatly reduced or destroyed the value of marshes as wildlife habitat, especially for muskrats and waterfowl, because the vegetation changes eliminated valuable food plants (Bourn and Cottam 1950).

The filling of marshes constitutes the greatest wetland loss in certain coastal areas, particularly those near urban centers. Much of the filling is done in small-scale, piecemeal fashion and generally goes unnoticed, except by individuals with immediate concern. Between 1954 and 1965, 45,000 acres were destroyed between Maine and Delaware (Teal and Teal 1969). The greatest single marsh loss to filling was caused by the disposal of spoil from *suction dredges* used to construct and maintain navigation channels for shipping. The suction dredge pumped water, silt, and sand from the channel into nearby diked areas that usually encompassed marshland. Water drained from the diked area and returned to the channel, but the silt and sand were retained and usually elevated the site several feet, thus destroying the marshland (Chapman 1968).

The U.S. Army Corps of Engineers annually dredges in excess of 280 million cubic yards of sediment for maintenance and improvement of waterways in the United States. Much of this dredging is in the coastal zone and past selections of spoil-disposal sites and methods were based mainly on economic criteria. However, environmental impact is now given careful consideration, and dredge spoil often is used to create or reestablish wetlands in bodies of shallow water (Smith 1977).

Much marsh has been filled by developers for construction of buildings, highways, airports, industrial complexes, and parking lots (Teal and Teal 1969). Also, urban planners usually consider local marshlands as ideal locations for city dumps, and thousands of acres have been filled with garbage.

Canal Dredging

Canals are dredged in coastal marshes for navigation, pipelines, drainage, and access to oil and gas-drilling sites. The size of canals varies with the purpose for which they were constructed. Small drainage ditches may be only 10 feet wide, but some navigation canals were constructed to accommodate oceangoing vessels and are several hundred feet wide. The length of canals also varies. Some access canals to drilling sites may extend into marshes only a few hundred feet; others may form an elaborate network of waterways. Ship channels and pipeline canals, on the other hand, may extend inland from the sea and cross the full expanse of marshes, often exceeding distances of 25 miles.

Canal construction causes a direct loss of coastal marshes in two ways. First, excavation changes the site from marshland to open water and greatly reduces its value as habitat for most wildlife. Second, the spoil removed by excavation is placed adjacent to the canal and converts that site from wetlands to an upland environment. Although spoil deposits and levees thus constructed represent a loss of wetland wildlife habitat, they provide terrestrial (high land) habitat and, in most instances, are used heavily by wildlife. Spoil deposits along canals support stands of shrubs and trees, add diversity to the area, and attract a wide array of wildlife species. Spoil deposits provide

Super highways and interchanges destroy much coastal marsh and facilitate development of remaining areas.

travel lanes, alternate feeding areas, upland nesting and brooding sites, and an elevated retreat during floods (Dell and Chabreck 1986).

After initial construction, canals continue to widen causing further land loss; the width of canals may double after a decade (Craig et al. 1979, Turner et al. 1982). Wave wash from boats causes shoreline erosion and the widening rate of canals is proportional to the amount of boat traffic. The nature of the marsh soil influences its susceptibility to erosion, and canal widening is directly related to the organic content of the substrate (Nichols 1958). The rate of erosion decreases with time and restricted use of canals can further reduce the widening rate.

Along the Louisiana coast, the acreage of canals is equal to 1.4% of the total marsh area (Craig et al. 1979). However, energy development is given a high national priority, and canal dredging for oil and gas development is continuing at a rapid rate (Turner et al. 1982). As the amount of marshland converted to open water by canal dredging increases, the acreage of marsh wildlife habitat will continue to decrease.

Saltwater Intrusion

Stratification of coastal marshes into distinct marsh types or vegetational communities has been maintained naturally by surface

Ship channels that extend far inland from the sea and transect coastal marshes sever natural tidewater barriers and permit highly saline water to reach fresher interior marshes.

features and hydrological processes. The inland advancement of seawater is usually restricted by natural barriers such as beaches, low marsh ridges, and natural levees along streams and lakes. Coastal streams meander and become narrower and shallower as they move inland, thus reducing their capacity to carry large volumes of saltwater. Also, the discharge of freshwater from inland sources through coastal streams serves to dilute and restrict the inland advancement of saline tidewater (Chapman 1973, Chabreck 1981).

Activities of humans including canal dredging and stream channelization coupled with natural processes such as subsidence, sea level rise, and shoreline erosion have reduced the effectiveness of saltwater barriers and altered hydrological patterns (Chabreck 1982a). Canals and channelized streams that connect tidal saline water sources to inland marshes of lower salinity function in two ways to alter marsh types. During periods of exceptionally low tides, canals facilitate drainage by lowering water levels in inland streams and lakes and flushing fresher water from interior marshes. Then, with ensuing high tides, saline water is able to flow in a more direct route farther inland. The process is gradual and is often interrupted when periods of heavy rainfall recharge freshwater sources. A period of several years may be necessary before the effects of saltwater intrusion become evident (Chabreck 1981).

As water salinity increases in a marsh, plants unable to tolerate the higher salinity die and are gradually replaced by species adapted to the new salinity regimes. Similarly, wildlife occupying the marsh because of preference for prevailing plants, gradually abandon the area (Chabreck 1982a, Fruge 1982). Also, wildlife intolerant to a saline environment, such as the alligator, will move inland with the retreating freshwater.

Greatest damage to plants and wildlife takes place when fresh marsh containing high levels of organic matter in the soil is subjected to saltwater and strong tidal action. When plants in the area are killed by increased water salinity, the organic substrate becomes loose and disorganized without plant roots to hold it together (Craig et al. 1979). With each tidal cycle, small amounts of organic matter are flushed out through tidal channels. Before plants adapted to the new conditions can become established, marsh elevations may be lowered enough to prevent growth of emergent plants. Open ponds and lakes are thus formed and productive marshland is lost (Chabreck 1981).

Studies along the Louisiana coast disclosed that 1,440 square miles (21.9% of the state's coastal marshland) were affected by salinity changes between 1968 and 1978. This included a 13.7% change to more saline vegetative types and an 8.2% change to less saline types for a net increase to more saline conditions on 5.5% of the total marsh area or 209 square miles. The change to less saline conditions was caused by record-breaking floods on the Mississippi River, the opening of spillways in the river's levee system, and the discharge of vast quantities of freshwater to the coastal marshes (Chabreck and Linscombe 1982).

CHAPTER 8
Marsh Management

The density of wildlife species occupying coastal marshes is largely regulated by the quality and quantity of available habitat. Individual species have specific habitat requirements and greatest populations occur when conditions are within the optimal range. However, the rapid loss and alteration of coastal marshes have reduced the quantity of habitat and caused habitat quality to deteriorate and wildlife populations to decline in most areas. As more demands are placed on coastal marshes in the future, the implementation of special management practices will become essential if the remaining wetland habitat is to be maintained at a level of high wildlife productivity (Sanderson and Bellrose 1969).

Most management practices are designed to improve habitats for wildlife classified as game and commercial species; however, habitat improvement for these groups benefits other wildlife as well. Game species in the coastal zone include ducks, geese, coots, rails, gallinules, snipe, rabbits, and white-tailed deer. Commercial wildlife species found in coastal marshes are the fur-bearing animals and the alligator. Past efforts at habitat management have been directed primarily at ducks and muskrats, but in some areas geese, nutrias, and alligators also receive major attention. Marshes along the Gulf and Atlantic coasts are major wintering areas for migratory ducks, and managers of private land work to improve habitat to attract ducks for the purpose of sport hunting. Numerous federal and state wildlife refuges and management areas are situated within the coastal zone, and habitat management is practiced to maintain and improve habitat quality for all wildlife.

Management Planning

Marsh management is costly and the benefit gained depends on the amount of money invested and the skill with which the program is planned. Unfortunately, marsh owners frequently launch development projects without fully understanding the problems they are trying to correct. Usually, planning by persons most familiar with the problems reduces the cost of a program and increases its effectiveness. Ecological processes in coastal marshes are complex and involve the action and interaction of numerous factors. The goal of management should be to manipulate these processes to produce the desired plant and animal communities (Chabreck 1975).

In planning a marsh management project, several factors should be carefully considered. First, establish management objectives that include priorities for the wildlife species to be produced in or attracted to the marsh. Optimal habitat for one species may not necessarily meet all requirements for another. Second, obtain detailed information on area environmental conditions such as water quality, water level fluctuation, soil characteristics, and climatic factors. Third, determine the wildlife value and growth requirements of common plants in the area. Fourth, fully understand wildlife habitat requirements and the factors affecting abundance of local wildlife (Chabreck 1976).

Rapidly deteriorating habitat conditions in most coastal marshes have greatly reduced their value to wildlife, and habitat improvement practices are necessary to increase production of resident species and serve the needs of migrant species. This can be accomplished by establishing favorable food and cover plants, regulating water depths to make food readily available, and creating a desirable marsh-to-water ratio (Weller and Spatcher 1965, Sanderson and Bellrose 1969). To accomplish these goals, habitat management should control water levels, stabilize water salinity, and minimize water turbidity.

Individual species of marsh and aquatic plants grow best when water depth and salinity remain within a limited range. In fact, several species with similar habitat requirements may concurrently occupy an area (a plant association). The marsh manager must identify the local plant association that best meets the food and cover requirements of the desired wildlife species and provide the range of water conditions that maximize growth of the plants. Without control of water depth and salinity, plants may be excessively exposed to conditions outside their tolerance limits, resulting in reduced growth or death. Moreover, less desirable species that are better suited to the changed conditions may invade the area.

Water turbidity is caused by dissolved or suspended materials and may affect growth of submersed aquatic plants by reducing water transparency. Silt-laden water that enters remote marsh ponds through tidal channels often eliminates stands of aquatic plants. Most aquatic plants are valuable wildlife foods and grow best when tidal flow into marsh ponds is restricted to reduce water turbidity.

All marsh types contain plant species that are important wildlife foods. However, abundance of these plants varies among localities, depending on local conditions such as elevation and drainage patterns. Salt marshes generally produce fewer plants that are preferred wildlife foods than other marsh types; consequently, reduction of water salinity is often necessary to maximize production. Also, certain carnivores, such as the alligator, occur mainly in low salinity or fresh areas and reduction of salinity is necessary to enhance productivity (Chabreck 1965, 1976).

Along the South Atlantic and Gulf coasts, the brackish zone is often managed to produce Olney bulrush, saltmarsh bulrush, waterhyssop, and dwarf spikerush in the marsh, and wigeongrass in ponds. Intermediate marshes of these regions usually are managed for wild millet, sprangletop, flatsedge, and other plants that produce an abundance of seeds for ducks. Pondweed and naiad are preferred aquatic plants. Plants favored in fresh-marsh management include smartweed, spikerush, and fall panicum; watershield, duckweed, and pondweed are important aquatic plants (Chabreck 1960, Neely 1962, Morgan et al. 1975).

Marshes in the early stages of plant succession generally have greater wildlife value than those in advanced stages, and measures should be implemented to "set back" succession or maintain early stages (Sanderson and Bellrose 1969). By controlling water depths and salinities, the marsh manager can usually promote the growth of desirable plants and control undesirable plants. Other treatments or control measures may also be necessary to protect habitats or develop

Wild millet and other plants that grow each year from seeds are important producers of food for ducks and many other birds. Drying of marshes during summer promotes seed germination and growth of the plants. Shallow flooding during winter facilitates feeding by dabbling ducks.

specific habitat conditions (O'Neil 1949, Baldwin 1968, Wilson 1968, Chabreck 1976).

Marsh Impoundments

Marsh *impoundments* are commonly used to manage marshes to improve wildlife habitat (Fig. 19). A marsh is considered impounded when completely surrounded by elevated land, including levees and natural ridges, that restricts water movement between the marsh and adjacent drainage systems. Water control structures such as *gated-culverts*, *stoplogs*, and pumps are placed in the impoundment levee at strategic locations and provide a means of adding or removing water (Chabreck 1960). An impoundment is a *closed system* and provides a mechanism for controlling water depth and salinity. Various management options are available with marsh impoundments (Fig. 20), and programs can be implemented to meet desired objectives (Morgan et al. 1975).

Impoundments can be managed as brackish or freshwater ecosys-

Dense stands of wigeongrass grow in brackish marsh ponds when the water is clear enough to permit penetration of light to the bottom. The plant is an important food of ducks wintering in coastal marshes.

Controlled burning is an important part of marsh management programs to encourage growth of Olney bulrush, a preferred food of muskrats and snow geese. Fall burns favor growth of the plant and reduce the danger of spring and summer wildfires that destroy nests and young of wildlife.

An alligator basking on a mat of dead vegetation. During early spring, alligators emerge from the water on sunny days and rest along the shoreline. When approached by humans, they hurriedly return to the water.

A suction dredge used to deepen a navigation channel removes mud from the bottom and pumps it through a long discharge pipe into a diked marsh on shore. Water dischargeed with the mud slowly drains back into the channel, but the mud remains and may raise the land inside the diked area several feet.

Canals dug for oil and gas exploration and production in coastal marshes increase the amount of open water, cover marshland with spoil deposits, and reduce the amount of wetland habitat for wildlife. However, spoil banks support stands of woody shrubs and provide wildlife with alternate feeding sites, travel lanes, upland nesting and brooding sites, and elevated retreats during floods.

Weirs in tidal streams stabilize water levels and prevent excessive drainage of marshes and ponds on low tides. Fish, shrimp, and blue crabs concentrate around the structures and attract sport fishermen.

Flocks of snow geese may contain a mixture of individuals of the white and blue color phases.

Young brown pelicans in a loosely constructed nest of twigs on a small shell mound. Egrets, herons, and ibises nest nearby in shrubs on a marshy island.

Locks on a navigation canal function as a barrier to the flow of highly saline tidewater to fresher interior marshes. Gates can be opened for passage of boats, drainage of excessive floodwaters, or ingress of marine organisms.

Migrant ducks concentrate during midwinter in a fresh-marsh impoundment that was drained the previous summer to promote germination and growth of seed-bearing grasses and sedges. Shallow flooding at depths less than 18 inches facilitates bottom feeding by the birds.

Muskrat lodges dot the landscape in a marsh of Olney bulrush.

Nutrias were introduced into the United States and are now common in Gulf and Atlantic coastal marshes. In Louisiana, nutrias have replaced muskrats as the state's leading fur producer.

tems with water maintained at constant levels or fluctuated seasonally (Chabreck 1960). By controlling water levels, the marsh manager can induce germination and growth of *annual plants* (Chabreck 1960, Baldwin 1968); attract birds to available food supplies (Sanderson and Bellrose 1969, Chabreck et al. 1974); control mosquitoes, fish, and

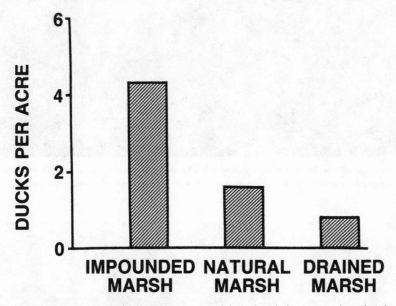

Figure 19. *Comparison of duck density in impounded marsh with that in natural marsh and marsh drained to establish cattle pasture (Chabreck et al. 1974).*

undesirable plants (Provost 1968, Chabreck 1960, Carney and Chabreck 1978); reduce water turbidity and promote growth of aquatic plants (Chabreck 1960); improve duck-brooding habitat (Allen 1981); enhance production of crayfish (Perry et al. 1970), improve habitat and food supplies for fur-bearing animals and alligators (Chabreck 1980); and accelerate marsh aggradation by reducing loss of organic material (SCS 1984).

Although marsh impoundments provide an effective means for improving wildlife habitat, impoundments can be constructed only in marshes having soils that will support a continuous levee system. Also, tidal channels and ponds in marshes are vital nursery areas for estuarine fisheries. Levees used for impounding marshes block normal

A water control structure of a marsh impoundment with stop-logs in place to regulate depth of flooding. Stop-logs can be removed to drain the area or permit ingress of postlarvae of marine organisms.

An impounded marsh managed for ducks lies to the right of the river and is well interspersed with clear-water ponds. Free-flowing tidal marsh to the left of the river has few open ponds, is flooded with turbid water on high tide, and provides low-quality habitat for ducks.

ingress and egress of aquatic organisms and reduce the size of the nursery area. Water control structures in impoundments at Rockefeller Wildlife Refuge in southwestern Louisiana are opened on high tide when postlarval and juvenile fishes and crustaceans are present, thus allowing them to enter the area. Young shrimp rapidly grow in the impoundments and are harvested by sport fishermen with cast nets several months later as the shrimp congregate at the structures to exit (Davidson and Chabreck 1983).

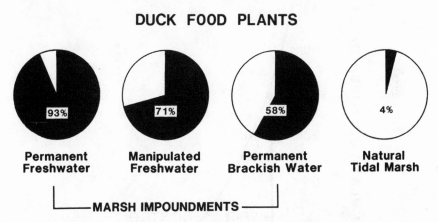

Figure 20. *Percentage of marsh flora comprised of duck food plants under different strategies of impoundment management (Chabreck 1960).*

Weirs and Plugs

An important technique for management of tidal marsh, particularly in areas that will not support a continuous impoundment levee, is construction of *weirs* in drainage systems of the marsh. A weir resembles a low dam constructed of steel or wooden *sheet piling*. The top or crest of the weir is normally placed 6 inches below the elevation of surrounding marsh, and water is allowed to flow back and forth across the structure (Chabreck and Hoffpauer 1962). *Earthen plugs* or dams also are placed across tidal streams and canals to block movement of water.

A weir reduces the rate of tidal flow and establishes a basin of water behind the structure which cannot recede below the crest; consequently, complete drainage of marshes and most ponds on low tide is prevented (Fig. 21). With reduced tidal flow, streams carry less suspended material and water turbidity decreases. The basin of water held by the weir functions as a mixing bowl and stabilizes water salinity (Chabreck and Hoffpauer 1962, Herke 1971, Chabreck et al. 1979).

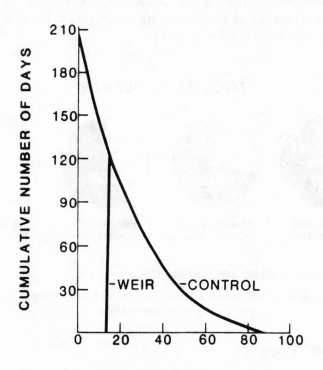

BOTTOM EXPOSURE (%)

Figure 21. *Cumulative number of days per year that ponds drained by free-flowing streams (control) and ponds stabilized by weirs will equal or exceed certain percentages of bottom exposure. Based on depth contours of 48 ponds and 20 years of tidal data on the central Louisiana coast (Chabreck et al. 1979).*

Hundreds of weirs have been constructed along the Louisiana coast for marsh management. Studies comparing ponds and lakes behind weirs with those drained by free-flowing streams disclosed that production of aquatic plants was 400% greater behind weirs (Chabreck 1968b). Weirs also increased use of ponds by ducks and improved habitat conditions for fur-bearing animals and alligators. Stabilized water levels improve access for trappers, hunters, and other visitors to a marsh (Spiller and Chabreck 1975).

Fish and crustaceans are able to move over a weir on incoming tides, but densities are usually less than those of free-flowing water bodies. Where fisheries production is part of a marsh management program, stocking densities can be increased by slightly lowering the weir crest or making other design modifications (Herke 1971, Rogers and Herke 1985). Fish, blue crabs, and shrimp concentrate around weirs and make the structures a favorite fishing site for marsh visitors (Davidson and Chabreck 1983).

Earthen plugs or dams also establish a permanent basin of water, but plug washouts are common and frequent maintenance is required. Studies have disclosed that growth of aquatic plants is not increased by damming tidal outlets. However, the structures prevent excessive marsh drainage, stabilize water levels in bayous and ponds, provide permanent water for ducks and other wildlife, and improve access by boat to interior marshes during low tides (Chabreck 1968). Earthen plugs block movement of fish and crustaceans but access to ponds and lakes is usually gained when high tides inundate the marsh. However, aquatic organisms are unable to exit because of the dam.

The most common use of earthen plugs in marsh management is to block canals not required for navigation. Pipeline canals and canals leading to abandoned oil and gas drilling sites often permit marsh drainage and saltwater intrusion. Damming the canals with earthen plugs effectively blocks water movement.

Potholes and Ditches

Artificial potholes (ponds) and small ditches provide habitat diversity in marshes with few natural openings and, in most instances, are beneficial to wildlife. Potholes and ditches provide permanent water and are particularly important during summer droughts to duck broods, fur-bearing animals, alligators, wading birds, frogs, and small fishes (Chabreck 1968b, Lynch 1968). Fish populations sustained in potholes and ditches during droughts help control mosquitoes when marshes are reflooded (Bowen and Cottam 1950).

Ditches are often placed in coastal marshes to provide water access to remote areas for trapping and hunting; however, several problems

Artificial potholes and ditches add habitat diversity to coastal marshes that have few natural openings. Ditches connected to tidal channels may drain the marsh excessively, allow saltier tidewater to enter, and alter composition of plant species.

Ditches provide trappers and hunters with access to remote sections of marsh and are a valuable source of water for fish and wildlife during extreme drought.

usually occur when ditches are connected to tidal streams. The ditches may cause excessive marsh drainage and changes in salinity regimes that ultimately affect wildlife populations by lowering habitat quality (Chabreck 1976).

Controlled Burning

Burning may be used under certain conditions to improve wildlife habitat in coastal marshes but should be used only in marshes where the area to be burned can be controlled. Also, marshes should be burned only during the fall and winter and to accomplish a specific objective. Spring and summer burns destroy nests and young of many species and should be avoided (Lynch 1941). However, lightning fires that often burn large areas are common during summer and cannot be controlled (O'Neil 1949).

Burning often is used in brackish marsh containing mixed stands of marshhay cordgrass and Olney bulrush to regulate species composition. Fall burns favor growth of Olney bulrush, an important wildlife food plant (Fig. 22), and without burning the plant is soon eliminated by the more dominant cordgrass (O'Neil 1949, Chabreck 1982b). Snow geese are attracted to burned marsh; small burns, properly spaced about a marsh and set at two-week intervals, provide ideal feeding areas for snow geese and keep birds in the locality (Lynch 1941). Nutrias, raccoons, and rails do not remain in burned areas because adequate cover is not available (Chabreck 1976).

Fresh and intermediate marshes should be burned only when encroachment of woody plants must be controlled; however, burning of salt marsh and spoil deposits should be avoided. The mixture of woody shrubs on spoil deposits provides important food and cover for wildlife and is killed by fire (SCS 1984). Before initiating a burning program in coastal marshes, the marsh manager should consider that most coastal zones are subsiding, sea levels are rapidly rising, and organic matter deposited by plants is a major source of material for marsh building. Fire will not only destroy the standing crop of vegetation, but when dry marsh is burned, organic material that has accumulated on the soil surface for many years may also be lost (Hackney and de la Cruz 1981, Hatton et al. 1983, SCS 1984).

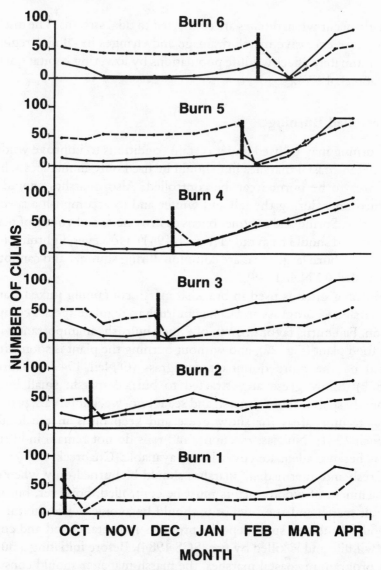

Figure 22. *Growth response of Olney bulrush (solid line) and marshhay cordgrass (broken line) to marsh burns at different dates (vertical bar) during fall, winter, and spring (Chabreck 1982).*

Food Plantings

One of the first procedures generally considered for improving wildlife habitat in a marsh is planting vegetation in the marsh to produce food. Such plantings are usually made without site preparation, and almost invariably the efforts fail to meet the desired objective. Usually the absence of natural food plants in a marsh is a result of unfavorable soil and water conditions or excessive competition from less-desirable plants. These conditions also cause the failure of plantings made in the same marsh area. Plantings in a marsh can never be a substitute for regulating water levels and salinities to produce natural foods. Only with the application of agronomic (agricultural) techniques have favorable results been achieved with artificial plantings on a large scale (Neely 1968).

Since Olney bulrush is a choice food plant of muskrats and snow geese in Atlantic and Gulf Coast marshes, there is considerable interest in managing marshes for this species. Procedures for establishing or reestablishing the species through planting have been the subject of intensive investigations (O'Neil 1949, Palmisano 1967, Ross and Chabreck 1972). The studies have disclosed that the species can be established by transplanting; however, plantings must be made within favorable water and salinity levels, protection must be provided against excessive competition from other plants, and animal disturbance must be controlled. Nutrias present the greatest problem and plantings must be made in fenced plots to be successful in marshes where the animals are abundant (Ross and Chabreck 1972).

Numerous plantings have been made in salt marshes for shoreline protection and dredge-spoil stabilization. Species used most were smooth cordgrass on the Atlantic and Gulf coasts and Pacific cordgrass on the west coast. Survival of plants used for shoreline protection was largely influenced by sediment grain size, wave severity, and shoreline configuration. Greatest survival occurred where fine sidement was present, wave height was minimal, and plantings were made in a sheltered cove (Knutson et al. 1981).

Cordgrass has been established on dredge spoil by direct seeding and transplanting. Success was obtained by direct seeding only in the upper portion of the *intertidal zone* and at higher elevations where seedlings could become firmly rooted. However, transplants were successful throughout the spoil area except where waves were severe or salinity excessive (greater than 45 ppt). Established stands of cord-grass were maintained longer where salinities remained about 20 ppt. The cost of establishing stands of cordgrass was greatly reduced where direct seeding could be used (Seneca 1980, Mason 1980).

Weed Control

Weeds have been defined as plants growing in areas where they are not wanted. A species may be a weed in one situation and a desirable plant in another. A plant may be considered a weed species in coastal wetlands managed for wildlife when wildlife use is reduced because it has low food and cover value, produces dense, impenetrable stands, or dominates other plants more useful to wildlife (Rollings and Warden 1964).

Control of undesirable plants over large areas may be best accomplished by regulating water levels (flooding or drying), burning, or grazing (Sanderson and Bellrose 1969). On small areas where these methods may not be possible or effective, herbicides are often very useful. Herbicides may be applied to create open ponds for ducks and other water birds, remove plants such as rattlebox and water hyacinth that overgrow ponds or drainage ditches, and eliminate dense vegetation around water-control structures. Before applying herbicides, the marsh manager should be aware of state and local regulations on herbicide use and select chemicals that are not harmful to fish and wildlife and have been cleared for use in wetlands. The herbicide used should be the best available for control of target plants and applied at recommended rates.

Restocking

The success of restoring populations of white-tailed deer, wild turkeys, and beavers in forested habitats by restocking has prompted interest in reestablishing other wildlife species in coastal wetlands using the same techniques. Restocking may be justified in areas with suitable habitat, where a species has been eliminated by overharvest or a catastrophic event such as a hurricane. In some cases, a population may not have been eliminated, but the number of individuals remaining may be so few that restocking is considered desirable to expedite recovery.

Restocking has been used with mixed success in attempts to reestablish muskrats, alligators, and brown pelicans in selected areas along the Louisiana coast. In all cases, areas selected as release sites contained ideal habitat for the species, but the population had declined to a level that justified restocking.

Marsh Island Wildlife Refuge along the central Louisiana coast contained an abundance of muskrats before Hurricane Audrey in 1957. A survey 8 months after the hurricane disclosed that vast Olney bulrush marshes were present, but no evidence of muskrats was found. Four hundred muskrats were then live-trapped elsewhere along the Louisiana coast and released on the island (Chabreck 1958). Several lodges appeared shortly after the release but soon disappeared and the effort was considered a failure. The cause of their disappearance could not be determined, and muskrats did not reappear on the area until 10 years later; however, their reappearance was not a result of the restocking effort.

Alligators were killed for their skin over a period of many years with practically no control on hunting and by 1960 the species was practically nonexistent along the Louisiana coast outside refuges and other protected areas. The season was closed and restocking was begun in southwestern Louisiana with animals removed from refuges. By 1962, 1,500 alligators were released in areas providing good habitat. No inventories were made of the areas before restocking, but by 1970 populations had greatly increased. Protection of remnant populations no doubt played an important role in the increase, but the restocking effort also contributed to the animal's return and was particularly important for gaining public support of the protection program (Chabreck 1965).

One of the most successful restocking programs was the effort to restore the brown pelican. As late as 1958, brown pelicans were abundant along the southeastern Louisiana coast and nested in shrubs on small marshy islands and isolated beaches. The birds began dying shortly thereafter and by 1962 no nesting birds were present in the state and only a few individuals remained. Their extermination was associated with contamination of the food chain by chlorinated hydrocarbons (probably the pesticide endrin) (Lowery 1974, Blus et al. 1975). The chemical curtailed reproduction by causing the birds to lay eggs with extremely thin shells that often broke in the nest. Also, many adult pelicans probably died from toxic effects of the compound (Lowery 1974, Cockerham 1984).

After contamination from the pesticide had subsided, a restocking program was initiated in 1968 by introducing *fledgling* (flightless young) brown pelicans from rookeries in Florida. Annual releases of 50 to 100 birds were made over a period of years resulting in successful reestablishment of the birds. Today, brown pelicans can again be seen nesting on the small islands and beaches (Cockerham 1984).

Kemp's ridley, the smallest and most colorfully marked of the Atlantic and Gulf sea turtles, ranges throughout the Gulf of Mexico and often appears along the Atlantic coast to New England (Conant 1975). The only known nesting site is at Rancho Nuevo along the eastern coast of Mexico. When the nesting site was discovered in 1947, over 40,000 Kemp's ridleys nested there; today fewer than 500 females come ashore to nest. The primary cause for the decline was predation, mainly by humans, though, raccoons, skunks, and birds eat the eggs or newly hatched turtles. Also, many adults are killed at sea when they are caught in trawls (Malone 1986).

The National Marine Fisheries Service and National Park Service have led a program to rebuild the Kemp's ridley population by establishing other nesting colonies. Assisted by many volunteers, eggs are collected at Rancho Nuevo, incubated, and the young are then released temporarily at a new site to imprint the site in their memory. As the young reach the Gulf, they are captured, returned to a hatchery, and reared in tanks for one year. After that time, they are much larger and stronger and are released offshore from the new site with hopes that they will return there to nest. Initial releases have been made on Padre Island, Texas, but other sites will be selected if the program meets with success (Malone 1986).

Animal Control

When wild or domestic herbivores, foraging animals, overpopulate marsh ranges, they often reduce plant density and alter species composition. The condition thus produced is not only detrimental to the overpopulated species, but to other wildlife as well. Muskrat and nutria populations increase in an area when marsh conditions are ideal. The increase is usually caused by a combination of factors including greater reproduction, improved survival, and movement of animals into the area. If the population increases beyond the carrying capacity of the marsh, vegetation eatouts often occur. The marsh manager should frequently monitor population levels and marsh conditions to prevent overpopulation. Surplus animals should be removed each winter through a systematic trapping program (Lynch et al. 1946, O'Neil 1949, Harris and Webert 1962).

Snow geese are gregarious creatures and a flock of several thousand birds may concentrate in a small area. If the geese remain in an area too long, they remove much of the vegetation and often create small lakes. Controlled burning of small plots nearby will usually attract the geese to other areas; however, if this fails, harassment may be necessary to move the birds to alternate sites (Lynch et al. 1946).

The effects of cattle grazing on wildlife in coastal marshes vary with the cattle-stocking rate, season, and wildlife species involved. Controlled grazing can be beneficial to ducks where marshes can be moderately grazed during spring and early summer to control plant growth, then flooded during the fall and winter to attract ducks. Cattle remove dense stands of mature vegetation, but if grazing is too light, control of plants that compete with duck-food-producing species may not be sufficient. However, if grazing is too heavy, cattle may reduce seed production in duck-food plants and kill other plants by trampling them (Neely 1958). Providing adequate cover is an important aspect of habitat management for wild mammals, and anything other than light grazing is usually detrimental (Chabreck 1968a).

Introduction of Freshwater

Reduction of freshwater flow to estuaries by damming and leveeing rivers or diverting a portion of their flow to other areas has drastically affected coastal marshes in most regions of the United States. Release of freshwater is needed to protect or restore the quality of estuaries and coastal marshes as fish and wildlife habitat (Chapman 1973). However, such a program would require considerable planning and public support for implementation and would face strong opposition from other water-user groups (Collins 1981).

Although not all estuaries are faced with the problem of reduced river flow, it is a critical problem confronting some of our largest and most productive estuarine systems such as Puget Sound (Rote 1981),

San Francisco Bay (Josselyn 1981), Florida Bay (Chapman 1973), Texas estuaries (Chapman 1973), and the Mississippi River delta (Craig et al. 1979). Water quality has also reached the critical stage in Chesapeake Bay, and more and more freshwater will be impounded or diverted in the future to meet increasing municipal and industrial needs. Unless political, social, and economic values are changed, important natural resources of the bay will continue to decline (Rote 1981).

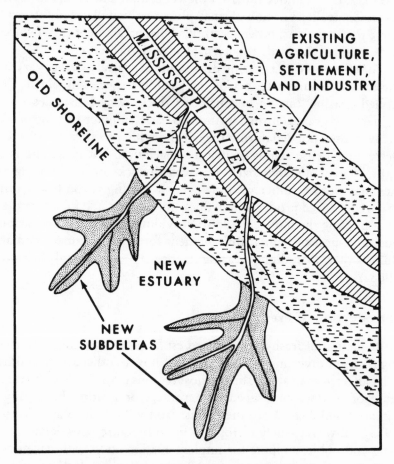

Figure 23. *New marshland could be created along the lower reaches of the Mississippi River by diverting river water through containment levees into shallow embayments. Careful spacing of controlled subdeltas also would create new estuaries (Gagliano et al. 1971).*

Introduction of freshwater from the Mississippi River through flood-protection levees into the marshes of southeastern Louisiana has been recommended as a procedure for reducing saltwater intrusion, enhancing plant growth, and improving wildlife habitat (Fruge 1982). Release of river water when it carries maximum sediment loads would not only function to reduce water salinity but would also promote preservation and building of marshes (Fig. 23). Controlled diversion of a portion of the river's flow during flood stages through strategically placed levee openings would result in formation of new subdeltas (Gagliano et al. 1971).

Protection of Barrier Islands

Barrier islands that line the outer reaches of the coastal zone buffer adjacent marshes from storms and regulate salinities (Fruge 1982). However, in many areas barrier islands are rapidly eroding and tidal passes between the islands, which function as control valves of the estuaries, continue to widen (Fig. 24) (Craig et al. 1979). Along the Louisiana coast, beach erosion may remove as much as 100 feet of land from barrier islands in one year (Penland et al. 1986).

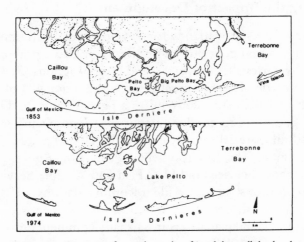

Figure 24. *Segments of coastal marshes fringed by well-developed beaches may become separated from the mainland by erosion and subsidence and form barrier islands. Without substantial input of coarse-grained sediment to help maintain these barriers, hurricanes and increased erosion from subsidence causes them to segment and gradually disappear (Penland and Boyd 1982).*

Efforts to rebuild and stabilize barrier islands in Louisiana received a supreme test in 1985 when three hurricanes (Danny, Elena, and Juan) struck the coast. Barrier island beaches were severely eroded by the hurricanes; but on a portion of Grand Isle, where a hurricane protection levee was recently constructed and beaches were raised with sand pumped in from offshore by the U.S. Army Corps of Engineers, damage was relatively minor. Also, on a portion of nearby Isle Dernieres, a parish-funded project that integrated sand nourishment and vegetation techniques offered most protection during the hurricanes (Penland et al. 1986).

With experience gained from the Grand Isle and Isle Dernieres projects, a Coastal Protection Plan will be implemented by the state to rebuild barrier islands elsewhere along the Louisiana coast. Restoration work will include the rebuilding of beaches and dunes with sand from offshore. Behind the dunes, large cellular retaining basins will be constructed and filled with sediment dredged from the bottom of bays behind the islands to form new marshland. Newly established dunes and marsh will be sodded with native plants as added protection against erosion.

Mitigating the Impact of Development

The use of coastal wetlands for developmental activities that involve filling, draining, or otherwise altering hydrological processes is regulated by various federal, state, and local programs (Zedler 1984). The primary federal involvement is through Section 404 of the Clean Water Act of 1972. This act requires a permit from the U.S. Army Corps of Engineers to conduct activities that result in discharge of dredge and fill material into "waters of the United States" (including coastal marshes). The Environmental Protection Agency, National Marine Fisheries Service, and U.S. Fish and Wildlife Service review permit applications and provide recommendations to the Corps regarding approval, denial, or modification of proposed activities. Also, state, local, and private groups usually comment on applications for permits (OTA 1984).

Any development in coastal marshes has the potential to adversely affect wildlife. However, the magnitude of impacts is site and project specific; a project at one site may produce minimal impacts but at another site the impacts of a similar project may be very destructive. Impact assessment is an important part of the permit-review process to determine which projects to allow in coastal wetlands and how to *mitigate* potentially adverse impacts (OTA 1984).

Mitigation measures usually are assigned as a condition of permit approval and require that specific actions be taken to minimize the impacts of a project on wetlands or to compensate for impacts resulting from the project. Both types of mitigation may be required for a project, but normally measures to compensate for impacts are required only where actions to minimize impacts would not be effective. Mitigation to minimize impacts associated with canal dredging in coastal marshes may include damming canals after project completion, backfilling canals in salt marsh (Gosselink 1984), or construction of weirs in small bayous transected by a canal. Mitigation to compensate for impacts of a project may require creation of new wetlands or improvement of existing wetlands at locations other than the project site (Zedler 1982).

Mitigation banking has been evaluated on a small scale but may be a means for encouraging private landowners to invest in costly marsh-management programs. Under this concept, the efforts of landowners to improve coastal wetlands for fish and wildlife can be quantified by designated public agencies and "banked" as "mitigation credits." Credits accumulated by this process can be used to mitigate unavoidable damages caused by developmental activities in the vicinity, subject to a case-by-case review by participating agencies (Arnett 1985).

Wildlife Refuges

Wildlife refuges are areas of land and water set aside and managed for the protection and preservation of native fauna and flora. They are managed in association with other land uses that do not conflict with their primary objective. Wildlife management areas and parks serve similar functions and may be established by public or private agencies (Gabrielson 1966).

The National Wildlife Refuge program began in 1903 when Pelican Island Refuge was established along the Florida coast to protect nesting habitat of brown pelicans and other colonial nesting birds (Salyer and Gillett 1964). The program rapidly advanced after that time and today practically all sections of the Gulf and Atlantic coastal regions contain areas set aside for conservation purposes.

Most refuges were established originally as sanctuaries for water-fowl to escape hunting pressure. However, management programs for refuges are now more habitat oriented and function to protect and improve habitat for all wildlife. Intensively managed marshes, such as those in wildlife refuges and wildlife management areas, will become increasingly important to wildlife in the future as more coastal marshes are lost or deteriorate.

CHAPTER 9

The Future
of Coastal Marshes

The Problem of Marsh Loss

Marshland along the nation's coasts is being lost at an alarming rate. Most of the loss involves conversion of marsh to open water, but in many instances, marshes have been diked and drained or covered with spoil to form dry land. Such losses have a great impact on wildlife that require a wetland environment for survival.

Human activities play a major role in marsh destruction. Ditching, canal dredging and spoil disposal were prominent activities for many years and have affected most coastal regions. The immediate loss of marshes to canal dredging was only a part of the problem. After construction, canal banks have continued to erode and additional marsh is lost as the channels widen. Also, many ditches and canals permit saltwater to move farther inland, thus destroying vegetation in fresher marsh zones.

Dams and levees along rivers that supply essential freshwater and land-building sediment to coastal marshes contribute to the loss. Freshwater input by rivers is necessary to maintain the natural horizontal zonation of marsh plant communities. Without adequate freshwater flow, seawater gradually encroaches inland, destroying fresher marsh vegetation as it advances. Of prime importance in the future is reestablishing freshwater flow from rivers to coastal marshes and estuaries.

Natural processes also contribute to the loss of coastal marshes.

High tides and strong currents associated with hurricanes erode shorelines, uproot marsh plants, and carry away floating marshes. Barrier islands often are segmented, badly eroded, and stripped of vegetative cover during the storms. Where land subsidence is progressing at a rapid rate, marshes are often inundated to such depths that plants are unable to survive; when the plants are lost, open lakes and embayments are formed.

Also of primary concern to coastal inhabitants is the rapidly accelerating rise in sea level. Predicted sea-level increases are 1 foot during the next 30 to 40 years and 3 to 5 feet during the next century (Titus 1985). If these predictions are correct, encroaching seas will destroy buildings, roads, airports, utilities, port facilities, and beaches; coastal grazing and cropland will be flooded; municipal water supplies will be contaminated with salt. However, the most severe consequence will be the erosion and inundation of thousands of square miles of coastal wetlands. Many natural tidewater barriers will be destroyed and saltwater will move far inland. Vegetation in interior marshes not destroyed by inundation will be killed by increased water salinity. Saltwater will also encroach into river valleys and forested wetlands will be adversely affected. Trees and woody shrubs adapted to freshwater environments will die (Titus et al. 1984a).

The rise and fall of sea level is nothing new in a geologic framework. The level of the sea has fluctuated 1,000 feet in the past and was 300 feet below its current position during the last ice age (18,000 years ago). Changes in sea level result from altered climatic conditions that cause slight changes in the earth's temperature. Past climatic changes were caused by natural factors; however, the recent modification, a warming trend first detected about 30 years ago, was induced by humans (Etkins and Epstein 1982).

Implementation of programs on a global basis to reverse the warming trend is unlikely. Therefore, coastal inhabitants must decide whether to protect property against the consequences of sea level rise or adapt to them. Problems associated with erosion, flooding, and saltwater intrusion must be addressed (Titus et al. 1984a). The efforts of marsh managers must be intensified if wildlife habitat is to be preserved.

Bald cypress killed by saltwater instrusion remain standing for many years and serve as a reminder of the drastic impact of coastal alteration.

Conflicting Land Uses

Early settlers used the coastal region for hunting, fishing, trapping, and livestock grazing with few land-use conflicts. As the human population increased, use of coastal marshes and adjacent waters also increased and the types of activity diversified. Current uses include residential and industrial development, agriculture, mineral extraction, and transportation, plus the traditional uses associated with fish and wildlife resources. Land-use conflicts are common and development in an area not only affects land uses in the area but also often affects land use in adjacent areas (Craig et al. 1979).

Current conflicts related to land use in the coastal zone provide some insight into conflicts to be faced in the future and the impact on fish and wildlife. Laws regulating wetland development now curtail certain types of activities in coastal marshes. However, some damages caused by previous development will magnify with time and result in further deterioration of fish and wildlife habitat. Erosion and saltwater intrusion associated with past canal dredging are current problems, and where corrective measures are not taken, the problems will become more severe as additional areas are affected.

As saltwater moves farther inland, the area of salt marshes con-

An oyster reef exposed along the shoreline of a tidal creek on low tide. Smooth cordgrass, the dominant plant of salt marshes along the Atlantic and Gulf coasts, grows into the intertidal zone.

tinues to expand and quality habitat for ducks and other wildlife that thrive in fresher environments decreases in size. The American oyster also is limited by saltwater intrusion because of the predacious oyster drill, a snail that occurs in water with a salt content over 15 ppt and kills oysters by drilling through their shells. Oyster growers are often forced to move their operations farther inland to less saline waters; however, those that relocate are soon faced with another water quality problem, domestic waste. Wastewater discharged from inland urban areas may have such high bacterial concentration that oysters exposed to the water become contaminated and cannot be marketed (Chapman 1973).

Some of our most productive coastal ecosystems are rapidly deteriorating because of competing uses. Water quality is a major factor affecting productivity of coastal waters in many areas, and contaminated water from areas in the drainage basin great distances from the coast may significantly contribute to the problem. Of particular concern are large basins, such as Chesapeake Bay, which encompass numerous political jurisdictions. Chesapeake Bay provides valuable habitat for fish and wildlife and also receives widespread use for transportation, recreation, and placement of wastes. Intensive competition among users and degradation of the system have rapidly escalated as the regional human population has increased. The drainage basin of Chesapeake Bay encompasses all or parts of six states, 138 counties, and the District of Columbia, thus making control of user activities a very difficult task. Any area within the basin may contribute significantly to the problems that affect the bay's productivity; therefore, programs to protect fish and wildlife habitat must include all political jurisdictions involved (Cronin 1981, Gottschalk 1981). Unfortunately, many political jurisdictions are unwilling to take the necessary measures to correct pollution problems that contribute to estuarine deterioration.

The problems of habitat deterioration caused by the vast array of competing uses of coastal marshes and waters are enough reason for concern. However, when the destruction caused by natural occurrences enters the picture, the problems magnify. We are unable to control natural losses caused by factors such as hurricanes and subsidence. Therefore, efforts must be made to control the activities of humans that contribute to further marsh destruction and to implement corrective measures to offset wetland losses and deteriorating habitat conditions caused by past activities. However, management efforts often provoke conflicts among affected interests and this can delay or reduce the effectiveness of corrective measures.

For more than 75 years, controlled diversion of Mississippi River water and sediment to estuarine areas of southeastern Louisiana has been recognized as essential to improve fish and wildlife habitat. The diversion would promote land building, enhance plant growth, and reestablish favorable salinity regimes. Implementation of the program is heavily dependent on involvement and support of a broad range of interests. However, during recent planning sessions, conflicts surfaced that further delayed the project. One group interested in the harvest of oysters and brown shrimp actually benefited from saltwater intrusion, since the harvest area expanded as saltwater moved farther inland into low salinity habitats. This group opposed freshwater diversion even though productivity over the entire area would actually be improved (Chatry and Chew 1985).

Another group recognized the need for freshwater diversion from the river but disagreed over the timing and magnitude of discharge. Salinity management schemes for waterfowl, fur-bearing animals, and alligators may not always be compatible with programs necessary to maximize production of estuarine fishes and crustaceans (Chatry and Chew 1985).

Most interest groups evaluate a management program by the immediate impacts on resources on which their livelihood or recreation depends, rather than by its overall value to the estuarine system. Further complicating restoration efforts is a long-standing federal policy that favors navigation and flood control over other uses of Mississippi River waters (Templet and Meyer-Arendt 1986). However, if effective management programs are to proceed, concessions must be made with the best interests of all resources in mind. A possible means for reaching a favorable consensus is to select a time period in the past considered acceptable by most interests, then implement carefully planned management programs to duplicate environmental conditions present at that time.

Recreational Needs

The pursuit of outdoor recreation increases each year as the population expands and Americans have more leisure time and greater mobility. By 1999, 75% of the U.S. population will live within 50 miles of the coastline, including the Great Lakes (Alexander et al. 1986); consequently, the coastal zone must satisfy a large part of the recreational demand. Seashores with broad, sandy beaches are a major public attraction. However, many individuals seek secluded marshes and estuaries of the coastal zone. Recreational uses of coastal marshes and estuaries include hunting, fishing, boating, birdwatching, photography, painting, nature study, archaeology, shell collecting, surfing, water skiing, and snorkeling (Davidson 1973, Reimold and Hardisky 1978).

Most large cities are faced with overcrowding and a shortage of open space (Jones and Sylvester 1978). However, many metropolitan areas near the coast are adjacent to marshes and estuaries that remain undeveloped and constitute a tremendous open-space resource with vast recreational potential. With careful planning, these areas can be developed to provide a diversity of recreational and educational facilities with minimum disturbance to their natural functions (Davidson 1973).

Many local governing bodies interested in promoting tourism have designated highways through coastal wetlands as scenic routes and have prepared tour-guide booklets that highlight points of interest along the routes. Pulloffs on the highways attract visitors and increase their safety. Pulloffs may have interpretative signs that identify major landscape features and plants and animals in the adjacent area. Further improvements may involve placement of descriptive nature trails and broadwalks. Parks and refuges may even provide guided tours along the borders of coastal marshes and tidal inlets.

Some coastal areas cannot accommodate unlimited crowds without destroying the very features that serve to attract visitors. Recreational areas should be operated with limits placed on public access in accordance with the natural capacity of the area. Point Lobos State Reserve along the California coast allows only a designated number of visitors at a time in order to protect a spectacular coastal *promontory*. Special

Coastal marinas facilitate recreational use of coastal marshes and estuaries, but dredging and filling for marina construction often destroys valuable fish and wildlife habitat.

protection may also be needed for delicate coastal features such as tidal pools, bluffs, and dune vegetation. As the recreational demand increases, additional sites should be added to prevent existing facilities from becoming overburdened (Bodovitz 1976).

Recreational boating has greatly increased in recent years and many coastal marinas are unable to meet the demand for berths. The marinas often were constructed in the past by dredging and filling valuable marshlands, thus destroying important fish and wildlife habitat (Bodovitz 1976, Gottschalk 1981). Such dredge-and-fill activities are now carefully regulated and generally prohibited; however, the demand for facilities still exists. Suggested solutions to the problem of providing additional boating opportunities while protecting valuable coastal wetlands are floating marinas in deeper water of natural harbors, dry storage, rental programs, and multiple ownership (Bodovitz 1976).

Meeting the recreational needs of the future will be an important task for public as well as private groups. Coastal marshes and estuaries with their abundance of living resources and unique habitats should play an important role in meeting these needs.

Coastal marshes historically have played an important role in providing the habitat of wetland wildlife and the recreational requirements and livelihood of humans; however, management programs implemented during the next decade may well determine the future of coastal marshes. Only with skillfully planned and promptly administered management programs can the marsh deterioration and loss caused by natural and human-induced forces be reversed. The cost of carrying out these programs will be high, but coastal marshes are an important part of our national heritage and well worth the efforts to save them.

APPENDIX A
Scientific Names of Animals and Plants

Alligator, American *Alligator missississippiensis*

Alligatorweed *Alternanthera philoxeroides*

Arrowgrass *Triglochin maritimum*

Arrowhead, Narrow-leaved *Sagittaria lancifolia*

Beaver *Castor canadensis*

Bass, Largemouth *Micropterus salmoides*

Bison *Bison bison*

Bladderwort *Utricularia* spp.

Bullfrog *Rana catesbeiana*

Bulrush *Scirpus* spp.

Bulrush, American *Scirpus americanus*

Bulrush, California *Scirpus californicus*

Bulrush, Olney *Scirpus olneyi*

Bulrush, Saltmarsh *Scirpus robustus*

Cattail *Typha* spp.

Coot, American *Fulica americana*

Cooter, Mobile *Chrysemys concinna mobilensis*

Cooter, Suwannee *Chrysemys concinna suwanniensis*

Cordgrass, Big *Spartina cynosuroides*

Cordgrass, Marshhay *Spartina patens*

Cordgrass, Pacific *Spartina foliosa*

Cordgrass, Smooth *Spartina alterniflora*

Cottonmouth *Agkistrodon piscivorus*

Cowpea, Hairypod *Vigna luteola*

Crab, Blue *Callinectes sapidus*

Crab, Fiddler *Uca pugnax*

Croaker, Atlantic *Micropogonias undulatus*

Crappie, Black *Pomoxis nigromaculatus*

Crayfish *Procambarus* spp.

Cypress, Bald *Taxodium distichum*

Deer, White-tailed *Odocoileus virginianus*

Drill, Oyster *Thais haemastoma*

Duck, Mottled *Anas fulvigula*

Duck Potato, Delta *Sagittaria platyphylla*

Duckweed *Lemna minor, Spirodela polyrhiza*

Eagle, Bald *Haliaeetus leucocephalus*

Eelgrass *Zostera marina*

Elephantsear *Colocasia antiquorum*
Fanwort *Cabomba caroliniana*
Flatsedge *Cyperus* spp.
Fleabane *Pluchea* spp.
Gadwall *Anas strepera*
Gallinule, Purple *Porphyrula martinica*
Glasswort *Salicornia* spp.
Goose, Canada *Branta canadensis*
Goose, Snow *Chen caerulescens*
Gull, Laughing *Larus atricilla*
Hairgrass, tufted *Deschampsia
cespitosa*
Harrier, Northern *Circus cyaneus*
Heron, Green-backed *Butorides
virescens*
Hornwort *Ceratophyllum demersum*
Hyacinth, Water *Eichhornia crassipes*
Hydrilla *Hydrilla verticillata*
Ibis, White-faced *Plegadis chihi*
Jaumea *Jaumea carnosa*
Limegrass *Elymus mollis*
Loosestrife, Swamp *Decodon ver-
ticillatus*
Mangrove, Black *Avicennia ger-
minans*
Menhaden, Gulf *Brevoortia patronus*
Millet, Wild *Echinochloa walteri*
Mink *Mustela vison*
Moorhen, Common *Gallinula
chloropus*
Muskrat *Ondatra zibethicus*
Naiad, Southern *Najas quadalupensis*
Nutria *Myocastor coypus*
Oak, Live *Quercus virginiana*
Otter, River *Lutra canadensis*
Oyster, American *Crassostrea vir-
ginica*
Panicum *Panicum* spp.
Panicum, Fall *Panicum
dichotomiflorum*
Panicum, Maidencane *Panicum
hemitomon*
Paspalum *Paspalum* spp.

Paspalum, Seashore *Paspalum
vaginatum*
Pelican, Brown *Pelecanus occidentalis*
Pennywort *Hydrocotyle* spp.
Pickleweed *Salicornia virginica*
Pintail, American *Anas acuta*
Pondweed *Potamogeton* spp.
Pondweed, Slender *Potamogeton
pusillus*
Rabbit, Marsh *Sylvilagus palustris*
Rabbit, Swamp *Sylvilagus aquaticus*
Raccoon *Procyon lotor*
Rail, Clapper *Rallus Longirostris*
Rail, King *Rallus elegans*
Rat, Rice *Oryzomys palustris*
Rattlebox *Sesbania drummondii*
Redfish or Red Drum *Sciaenops
ocellata*
Reed, Common *Phragmites australis*
Ridley, Kemp's *Lepidochelys kempi*
Rush, Needle *Juncus roemerianus*
St. Johnswort, Marsh *Hypericum
virginicum*
Saltgrass *Distichlis spicata*
Saltwort *Batis maritima*
Sawgrass *Cladium jamaicensis*
Sea-oxeye *Borrichia frutescens*
Seatrout, Spotted *Cynoscion nebulous*
Sedge, Star *Dichromena colorata*
Shrimp, Brown *Penaeus aztecus*
Shrimp, White *Penaeus setiferus*
Silverweed, Pacific *Potentilla pacifica*
Smartweed *Polygonum* spp.
Snake, Atlantic Salt Marsh *Nerodia
fasciata taeniata*
Snake, Gulf Salt Marsh *Nerodia fas-
ciata clarki*
Snake, Mangrove Water *Nerodia
fasciata compressicauda*
Snipe, Common *Capella gallinago*
Sparrow, Seaside *Ammospizo
maritima*
Spikerush *Eleocharis* spp.

Spikerush, Dwarf *Eleocharis parvula*
Sprangletop *Leptochloa* spp.
Swallow, Cliff *Petrochelidon pyrrhonota*
Teal, Blue-winged *Anas discors*
Tern, Caspian *Hydroprogne caspia*
Tern, Forster's *Sterna forsteri*
Tern, Royal *Thalasseus maximus*
Terrapin, Diamondback *Malaclemys terrapin*
Treefrog, Pacific *Hyla regilla*
Turkey, Wild *Meleagris gallopavo*
Turnstone, Ruddy *Arenaria interpres*
Turtle, Snapping *Chelydra serpentina*

Warbler, Yellow-rumped *Dendroica coronata*
Waterchestnut *Trapa natans*
Waterhyssop, Coastal *Bacopa monnieri*
Waterlily, Fragrant *Nymphaea odorata*
Watermilfoil, Eurasian *Myriophyllum spicatum*
Watershield *Brasenia schreberi*
Wigeongrass *Ruppia maritima*
Willet *Catoptrophorus semipalmatus*
Willow, Black *Salix nigra*
Yellowlegs, Greater *Tringa melanoleuca*

APPENDIX B
Glossary

Accrete. To grow in size or extent.

Aggrade. To raise the level or elevation.

Agronomic. Related to growing domestic crops.

Alluvial. Pertaining to sand, mud, etc., deposited by a flowing stream.

Anadromous. Going up a river from the sea to spawn.

Annual plant. A plant with a life span of one year.

Aquatic plant. A plant that lives and grows only in water.

Association. A community that consists of a characteristic combination of species.

Autotroph. Plant that manufactures its own nutritive substances by photosynthesis.

Backfill. To return soil or other material into the space from which it was removed.

Barrier Island. A long, narrow offshore island consisting of sand, gravel or shells and lying parallel to the coastline.

Biodiversity. The number of species of plants and animals in a community.

Browse. Tender shoots or twigs of shrubs and trees used as food by animals.

Carnivore. An organism that consumes mainly flesh.

Carrying capacity. The maximum number of a species that can be supported indefinitely by a particular area.

Cast net. A circular net that is thrown into the water for capturing fish and other aquatic organisms.

Cat clay. A soil condition that results occasionally when marshes are dried and chemical changes take place that produce sulfuric acid.

Chenier. An ancient beach deposit left stranded in a marsh by seaward advancement of the marsh.

Cline. A characteristic or feature of a species that grades along a line of environmental or geographic transition.

Closed system. A functional area that is mostly isolated because of barriers that exclude certain outside influences.

Colonize. To become established as a group in a new area.

Community. A group of different species occupying a particular area.

Continental shelf. The bottom of the relatively shallow portion of the seas fringing a continent.

Debris. The remaining parts from dead plants and animals.

Delta. The flat plain of alluvial deposits between diverging branches of the mouth of a river.

Dendritic. Having branches like a tree.

Detritivore. An organism that feeds on partially decomposed plant material.

Dicotyledon. A plant with two cotyledons or seed leaves.

Direct seeding. Planting by distributing seeds over an area.

Distributary. A branch of a stream that flows away from the main channel.

Diversity. Variety; the number of species of plants or animals in a community.

Drowned marshes. Marshes that have become permanently inundated by the sea.

Earthen plug. A dam constructed of earth.

Eatout. An area where all vegetation has been removed primarily by animal consumption.

Ecosystem. A community and its habitat functioning as an ecological unit.

Ecotone. A transition zone between two communities.

Edaphic. Relating to soil or topography.

Egress. To move out of an area.

Emergent plant. A plant capable of growing when rooted in flooded substrate but the photosynthetic parts of which must stand above the surface of the water.

Estuary. An arm of the sea, often semienclosed, where freshwater and saltwater mix.

Exotic. Of foreign origin.

Facultative halophyte. A plant that is salt tolerant but reaches optimum development in nonsaline soil.

Fledgling. A young bird not yet able to fly.

Flotant. A floating marsh.

Game. Wild animals hunted for sport or food.

Gated-culvert. A movable barrier in a pipe that can be opened or closed to regulate the flow of water.

Glycophyte. A plant capable of growing only in a nonsaline environment.

Greenhouse effect. A gradual warming of the earth's temperature caused by increased concentrations of carbon dioxide in the atmosphere and a reduction in the amount of solar heat escaping back into space.

Gregarious. Living in groups.

Halophyte. A salt-tolerant plant.

Haze. To subject to unusual and frightening disturbances.

Herbicide. A manufactured poison used to kill unwanted plants.

Herbivore. An organism that consumes mainly plant tissue.

Heterotroph. Incapable of manufacturing proteins and carbohydrates.

Holocene. The period of the Human or Recent era; post-Pleistocene geologic epoch.

Horizontal zonation. Organization on the ground surface into somewhat parallel bands of plant associations.

Hypersaline. Having a salinity greater than the usual strength of seawater.

Impoundment. Reservoir.

Imprint. To irreversibly fix in memory while an animal is very young.

Ingress. To move into an area.

Intertidal zone. The area between the high-tide mark and the low-tide mark.

Lateral. Pertaining to the side.

Marina. An area offering dockage and other services for small boats.

Meander. To proceed by a winding course.

Mesosaline. In the middle range of salinity.

Mineral. A substance occurring in nature such as sand, silt, and clay, not derived from plant or animal remains.

Mitigate. To moderate the severity of an impact or compensate for loss.

Mitigation banking. Improvements to fish and wildlife habitat that can later be used as a trade-off on other projects nearby that are detrimental to habitat because of unavoidable adverse impacts.

Monocotyledon. A plant with one cotyledon or seed leaf; typically elongated and grasslike.

Monotypic. Consisting primarily of one type or species.

Obligatory halophyte. A plant capable of growing only under saline conditions.

Oligosaline. In the low range of salinity.

Omnivore. An organism that eats both plant and animal tissue.

Opportunistic. Taking advantage of objects most readily available.

Organic. Derived from plants or animals.

Osmotic pressure. The pressure exerted against a semipermeable membrane by the movement of water through the membrane to an area of higher salt concentration.

Oxidation. A chemical change involving the addition of oxygen, often increasing the action of microorganisms that cause decay.

Photosynthesis. The process by which green plants in the presence of sunlight convert carbon dioxide and water into simple sugar.

Piecemeal. Fragmented into a number of smaller parts or projects.

Pleistocene. The epoch in earth's history that precedes the Holocene and is referred to as the Ice Age.

Postlarva. The early juvenile stage of crustaceans.

Pothole. A deep pond that is somewhat cylindrical.

Precocial. Able to move about freely soon after birth or hatching.

Preferential halophyte. A plant that is capable of growth in saline or nonsaline soil but reaches optimum development in saline soil.

Primary consumer. An animal that feeds on plants.

Primary productivity. The amount of organic matter produced by green plants.

Promontory. A high point of land or rock projecting into the sea.

Propagule. A seed, root, or other part of a plant that allows the plant to reproduce.

Rhizome. An underground stem used for reproduction and food storage.

Richness. The abundance of species in a community.

Secondary consumer. An animal that feeds on herbivores.

Sheet piling. A panel of steel or wood driven vertically into the ground to form a wall.

Shoal. An elevated region in the bottom of a water body and often exposed during low tides.

Spawn. The eggs of fishes and amphibia; to deposit eggs.

Spit. A long narrow point of land projecting into the water.

Spoil deposit. A mound of soil constructed by dredging.

Stoplogs Short boards placed in a slotted frame and mounted on the end of a drainpipe to regulate water depth.

Subdelta. A small delta that develops as a segment of a large delta.

Subsidence. A gradual sinking of the earth's surface.

Succession. The replacement of one community by another.

Suction dredge. A large, floating machine for removing soil and sediment from the bottom of a water body by means of a suction pipe.

Terrestrial. Living or growing on land.

Tertiary. A stage in the processing of sewage beyond secondary treatment to further improve water quality.

Transient. An individual that remains in an area for only a short time.

Trellis. A drainage system characterized by sharp turns to one side and then to the other.

Trophic. Pertaining to food or nutrition.

Tundra. A treeless plain of the arctic region dominated by mosses, sedges, and lichens.

Turbidity. Dissolved or suspended matter in water that reduces transparency.

Weir. A low dam placed across a stream to prevent excessive drainage without completely blocking the flow of water or movement of organisms.

APPENDIX C
Conversion Table

Metric to U.S. Customary

Multiply	By	To Obtain
millimeters (mm)	0.03937	inches
centimeters (cm)	0.3937	inches
meters (m)	3.281	feet
Kilometers (km)	0.6214	miles
square metres (m^2)	10.76	square feet
square kilometers (km^2)	0.3861	square miles
hectares (ha)	2.471	acres
liters (l)	0.2642	gallons
cubic meters (m^3)	35.31	cubic feet
cubic meters	0.0008110	acre-feet
milligrams (mg)	0.00003527	ounces
grams (g)	0.03527	ounces
kilograms (kg)	2.205	pounds
metric tons (t)	2205.0	pounds
metric tons	1.102	short tons
kilocalories (kcal)	3.968	British thermal units
degrees Celsius	1.8(C°) + 32	degrees Fahrenheit

U.S. Customary to Metric

inches	25.40	millimeters
inches	2.54	centimeters
feet (ft)	0.3048	meters
fathoms	1.829	meters
miles (mi)	1.609	kilometers
nautical miles (nmi)	1.852	kilometers
square feet (ft^2)	0.0929	square meters
acres	0.4047	hectares
square miles (mi^2)	2.590	square kilometers
gallons (gal)	3.785	liters
cubic feet (ft^3)	0.02831	cubic meters
acre-feet	1233.0	cubic meters
ounces (oz)	28.35	grams
pounds (lb)	0.4536	kilograms
short tons (ton)	0.9072	metric tons
British thermal units (BTUs)	0.2520	kilocalories
degrees Fahrenheit	$0.5556(F°) - 32$	degrees Celsius

References

References

Alexander, C. E., M. A. Boutman, and D. W. Field. 1986. An inventory of coastal wetlands of the USA. U.S. Dept. of Commerce. Washington, D.C. 25pp.

Allen, J. A. 1981. Nesting and productivity of mottled ducks in the marshlands of southwestern Louisiana. M.S. thesis. La. State Univ., Baton Rouge. 101 pp.

Arnett, G. R. 1985. Keynote speech. Pp. 1–6 in Bryan, C. F., P. J. Zwank, and R. H. Chabreck (eds.). Proc. 4th Coastal Marsh and Estuary Manage. Symp., La. State Univ., Baton Rouge.

Arthur, S. C. 1931. The fur animals of Louisiana. La. Dept. of Cons. Bull. 18, New Orleans. 444 pp.

Baldwin, W. P. 1968. Impoundments for waterfowl on South Atlantic and Gulf coastal marshes. Pp. 127–33 in Newsom, J. D. (ed.). Proc. Marsh and Estuary Manage. Symp., La. State Univ., Baton Rouge.

Bateman, H. A., Jr. 1965. Clapper rail (Rallus longirostrus) studies on Grand Terre Island, Jefferson Parish, Louisiana. M.S. thesis, La. State Univ., Baton Rouge. 145 pp.

Baumann, R. H. and R. D. DeLaune. 1982. Sedimentation and apparent sea level rise as a factor affecting land loss in coastal Louisiana. Pp. 2–13 in Boesch, D.W. (ed.). Proc. Conf. on Coastal Erosion and Modification in La.: Causes, Consequences, and Options. U.S. Fish and Wildl. Serv., FWS/OBS-82/59. Washington, D.C.

Blus, L. J., T. Joanen, A. A. Belisle, and R. M. Prouty. 1975. Brown pelicans and certain environmental pollutants in Louisiana. Bull. Environ. Contam. Toxicol. 13:646–55.

Bodovitz, J. E. 1976. California's coastal management plan. Trans. N. Am. Wildl. and Nat. Resources Conf. 41:237–55.

Boesch, D. F., D. Levin, D. Nummedal, and K. Bowles. 1983. Subsidence in coastal Louisiana: causes, rates, and effects on wetlands. U.S. Fish and Wildl. Serv., FWS/OBS-83/26. Washington, D.C. 30 pp.

Bourn, W. S. and C. Cottam. 1950. Some biological effects of ditching tidewater marshes. U.S. Fish and Wildl. Serv. Research Rep. 19. Washington, D.C. 30 pp.

Brannon, J. M. 1973. Seasonal variation of nutrients and physicochemical properties in the salt marsh soils of Barataria Bay, Louisiana. M.S. thesis. La. State Univ., Baton Rouge. 130 pp.

Brantly, R. M. 1980. The changing resource scene in Florida. Trans. N. Am. Wildl. and Nat. Resources Conf. 45:5–10.

Broley, C. L. 1947. Migration and nesting of Florida bald eagles. Wilson Bull. 59:3–20.

Buller, R. J. 1964. Central Flyway. Pp. 209–32 *in* Linduska, J. P. (ed.). Waterfowl Tomorrow. U.S. Fish and Wildl. Serv. Washington, D.C.

Carney, D. F. and R. H. Chabreck. 1977. An evaluation of spring drawdown as a waterfowl management practice in floating fresh marsh. Proc. Ann. Conf. Southeast. Assoc. Fish and Wildl. Agencies 31:266–71.

Carver, D. C. 1965. Ecological factors affecting distribution and abundance of the centrarchids of the recent delta of the Mississippi River. M.S. thesis. La. State Univ., Baton Rouge. 119 pp.

Chabreck, R. H. 1958. Muskrat transplanting. Biennial Rep. La. Wild. Life and Fish. Comm., New Orleans, 7:61–62.

Chabreck, R. H. 1960. Coastal marsh impoundments for ducks in Louisiana. Proc. Ann. Conf. Southeast. Assoc. Game and Fish Comm. 14:24–29.

Chabreck, R. H. 1965. Movement of alligators in Louisiana. Proc. Ann. Conf. Southeast. Assoc. Game and Fish Comm. 19:102–10.

Chabreck, R. H. 1966. Methods of determining the size and composition of alligator populations in Louisiana. Proc. Ann. Conf. Southeast. Assoc. Game and Fish Comm. 20:105–12.

Chabreck, R. H. 1968a. The relation of cattle and cattle grazing to marsh wildlife and plants in Louisiana. Proc. Ann. Conf. Southeast. Assoc. Game and Fish Comm. 22:55–58.

Chabreck, R. H. 1968b. Weirs, plugs, and artificial potholes for the management of wildlife in coastal marshes. Pp. 178–92 *in* Newsom, J. D. (ed.). Proc. Marsh and Estuary Manage. Symp., La. State Univ., Baton Rouge.

Chabreck, R. H. 1970. Marsh zones and vegetative types in the Louisiana coastal marshes. Ph.D. dissertation. La. State Univ., Baton Rouge, 112 pp.

Chabreck, R. H. 1971. Ponds and lakes of the Louisiana coastal marshes and their value to fish and wildlife. Proc. Ann. Conf. Southeast. Assoc. Game and Fish Comm. 25:206–15.

Chabreck, R. H. 1972. Vegetation, water and soil characteristics of the Louisiana coastal region. La. Agr. Exp. Sta. Bull. 664. Baton Rouge. 72 pp.

Chabreck, R. H. 1975. Waterfowl management and productivity—Gulf coast habitat. Int. Waterfowl Symp., Ducks Unlimited, Chicago, 1:64–72.

Chabreck, R. H. 1976. Management of wetlands for wildlife habitat improvement. Pp. 226–33 *in* Wiley, M. (ed.). Estuarine Processes: Uses, Stresses, and Adaptation to the Estuary. Vol. 1. Academic Press, New York.

Chabreck, R. H. 1979. Wildlife harvests in wetlands of the United States. Pp. 618–31 *in* Greeson, P.E., J. R. Clark, and J. E. Clark (eds.). Wetland Functions and Values: the State of Our Understanding. Am. Water Resour. Assoc., Minneapolis.

Chabreck, R. H. 1980. Effects of marsh impoundments on coastal fish and wildlife resources. Pp. 1–16 *in* Fore, P. L. and R. D. Peterson (eds.). Proc. Gulf of Mexico Coastal Ecosystems Workshop. U.S. Fish and Wildl. Serv., FWS/OBS-80/30. Washington, D.C.

Chabreck, R. H. 1981. Freshwater inflow and salt water barriers for management of coastal wildlife and plants in Louisiana. Pp. 125–38 *in* Cross, R. D. and D. L. Williams (eds.). Proc. Nat. Symp. on Freshwater Inflow to Estuaries. Vol. 2. U.S. Fish and Wildl. Serv., FWS/OBS-81/04. Washington, D.C.

Chabreck, R. H. 1982a. The effect of coastal alteration on marsh plants. Pp. 92–98 *in* Boesch, D. F. (ed.). Proc. Conf. on Coastal Erosion and Wetland Modification in Louisiana: Causes, Consequences, and Options. U.S. Fish and Wildl. Serv., FWS/OBS-82/59. Washington, D.C.

Chabreck, R. H. 1982b. Effect of burn date on regrowth rate of *Scirpus olneyi* and *Spartina patens*. Proc. Ann. Conf. Southeast. Assoc. Fish and Wildl. Agencies 35:201–10.

Chabreck, R. H., F. J. Hoar, and W. D. Larrick, Jr. 1979. Soil and water characteristics of coastal marshes influenced by weirs. Pp. 127–46 *in* Day, J. W., Jr., D. D. Culley, Jr., R. E. Turner, and A. J. Mumphrey, Jr. (eds.). Proc. 3rd Coastal Marsh and Estuary Manage. Symp., La. State Univ., Baton Rouge.

Chabreck, R. H. and C. M. Hoffpauer. 1962. The use of weirs in coastal marsh management in Louisiana. Proc. Ann. Conf. Southeast. Assoc. Game and Fish Comm. 16:103–12.

Chabreck, R. H. and R. G. Linscombe. 1982. Changes in vegetative types in the Louisiana coastal marshes over a 10-year period. Proc. La. Acad. Sci. 45:98–102.

Chabreck, R. H. and A. W. Palmisano. 1973. The effects of hurricane Camille on the marshes of the Mississippi River delta. Ecology 54:1118–23.

Chabreck, R. H., R. K. Yancey, and L. McNease. 1974. Duck usage of management units in the Louisiana coastal marshes. Proc. Ann. Conf. Southeast. Assoc. Game and Fish Comm. 28:468–74.

Chambers, D. G. 1980. An analysis of nekton communities in the upper Barataria basin, Louisiana. M.S. thesis. La. State Univ., Baton Rouge. 286 pp.

Chapman, C. 1968. Channelization and spoiling in Gulf Coast and South Atlantic estuaries. Pp. 93–106 in Newsom, J. D. (ed.). Proc. Marsh and Estuary Manage. Symp., La. State Univ., Baton Rouge.

Chapman, C. R. 1973. The impact of estuaries and marshes of modifying tributary runoff. Pp. 235–58 in Chabreck, R. H. (ed.). Proc. 2nd Coastal Marsh and Estuary Manage. Symp., La. State Univ., Baton Rouge.

Chapman, V. J. 1960. Salt marshes and salt deserts of the world. Interscience Publishers, New York. 392 pp.

Chatry, M. and D. Chew. 1985. Freshwater diversion in coastal Louisiana: recommendations for development of management criteria. Pp. 71–84 in Bryan, C. F., P. J. Zwank, and R. H. Chabreck (eds.). Proc. 4th Coastal Marsh and Estuary Manage. Symp., La. State Univ., Baton Rouge.

Clark, J. 1974. Coastal ecosystems—ecological considerations for management of the coastal zone. The Conservation Found., Washington, D.C. 178 pp.

Cockerham, M. N. 1984. A "Wunnerfull" bird is the pelican. La. Conservationist 36(4):8–11.

Coleman, J. M. 1966. Recent coastal sedimentation: Central Louisiana Coast. Coastal Studies Series No. 17, La. State Univ. Press. Baton Rouge. 73 pp.

Collins, K. 1981. Problems of freshwater inflow planning in California. Pp. 62–63 in Cross, R. and D. Williams (eds.). Proc. Nat Symp. on Freshwater Inflow to Estuaries. Vol. 1. U.S. Fish and Wildl. Serv., FWS/OBS-81/04. Washington, D.C.

Conant, R. 1975. A field guide to reptiles and amphibians of eastern and central North America. Houghton Mifflin, Boston. 429 pp.

Copeland, B. J., R. G. Hodson, S. R. Riggs, and J. E. Easley. 1983. The ecology of Albemarle Sound, North Carolina: an estuarine profile. U.S. Fish and Wildl. Serv., FWS/OBS-83/01. Washington, D.C. 68 pp.

Correll, D. S. and H. B. Correll. 1972. Aquatic and wetland plants of the southwestern United States. U.S. Environ. Protection Agency, Washington, D.C. 1777 pp.

Cowardin, L. M., V. Carter, F. C. Golet, and E. T. LaRoe. 1979. Classification of wetlands and deepwater habitats of the United States. U.S. Fish and Wildl. Serv., FWS/OBA-79/31. Washington, D.C. 103 pp.

Craig, N. J., R. E. Turner, and J. W. Day, Jr. 1979. Land loss in coastal Louisiana (U.S.A.). Environmental Manage. 3(2):133–44.

Cronin, L. E. 1981. The Chesapeake Bay. Trans. N. Am. Wildl. and Nat. Resources Conf. 46:223–29.

Dachnowski-Stokes, A. P. 1940. Structural characteristics of peats and mucks. Soil Science 50:389–400.

Davidson, G. 1973. Meeting the needs for recreation opportunity in marsh and estuarine areas.

Pp. 295–306 *in* Chabreck, R. H. (ed.). Proc. 2nd Coastal Marsh and Estuary Manage. Symp., La. State Univ., Baton Rouge.

Davidson, R. B. and R. H. Chabreck. 1983. Fish, wildlife, and recreational values of brackish marsh impoundments. Pp. 89–114 *in* Varnell, R. J. (ed.). Proc. Water Qual. and Wetlands Manage. Conf., New Orleans.

de la Cruz, A. A. 1978. Production and transport of detritus in wetlands. Pp. 162–74 *in* Greeson, P. E., J. R. Clark, and J. E. Clark (eds.). Wetland Functions and Values: The State of Our Understanding. Amer. Water Resources Assoc., Minneapolis.

Dell, D. A. and R. H. Chabreck. 1986. Levees and spoil deposits as habitat for wild mammals in the Louisiana coastal marshes. School For., Wildl., and Fish. Res. Rep. No. 7, Baton Rouge. 47 pp.

Edelman, C. H. and J. M. van Staveren. 1958. Marsh soils in the United States and in The Netherlands. J. Soil and Water Cons. 13:5–17.

Emery, K. O. and E. Uchupi. 1972. Western North Atlantic Ocean: topography, rocks, structures, water, life, and sediments. Memoir 17. Amer. Assoc. of Petroleum Geologists. Tulsa, Okla. 532 pp.

Ensminger, A. and G. Linscombe. 1980. The fur animals, the alligator, and the fur industry in Louisiana. La. Dept. of Wildl. and Fish. Baton Rouge. 69 pp.

Ensminger, A. B. and L. G. Nichols. 1957. Hurricane damage to Rockefeller Refuge. Proc. Ann. Conf. Southeast. Assoc. Game and Fish Comm. 11:52–56.

Etkins, R. and E. Epstein. 1982. The rise in global sea level as an indication of climatic change. Science 215:287–98.

Fleming, D. M. 1975. Movement patterns of the coastal marsh raccoon in Louisiana and notes on its life history. M.S. thesis. La. State Univ., Baton Rouge. 90 pp.

Fruge, D. W. 1982. Effects of wetland deterioration on the fish and wildlife resources of coastal Louisiana. Pp. 99–107 *in* Boesch, D. F. (ed.). Proc. Conf. on Coastal Erosion and Modification in La.: Causes, Consequences, and Options. U.S. Fish and Wildl. Serv., FWS/Obs-82/59. Washington, D.C.

Gabrielson, I. N. 1966. Wildlife conservation. Macmillian, New York. 244 pp.

Gagliano, S.W., P. Light, and R. E. Becker. 1971. Controlled diversion in the Mississippi delta system: an approach to environmental management. Center for Wetland Resources Rep. No. 8, La. State Univ., Baton Rouge. 146 pp.

Gagliano, S. W., K. J. Meyer-Arendt, and K. M. Wicker. 1981. Land loss in the Mississippi Deltaic Plain. Trans. Ann. Meeting Gulf Coast Geol. Soc. 31:295–300.

Gallagher, J. L. 1980. Salt marsh soil development. Pp. 28–34 *in* Lewis J. C. and E. W. Bunce (eds.). Rehabilitation and Creation of Selected Coastal Habitats: Proceedings of a Workshop. U.S. Fish and Wildl. Serv., FWS/OBS-80/27. Washington, D.C.

Gosselink, J. G. 1980. Tidal marshes—the boundary between land and ocean. U.S. Fish and Wildl. Serv., FWS/OBS-80/15. Washington, D.C. 13 pp.

Gosselink, J. G. 1984. The ecology of delta marshes of coastal Louisiana: a community profile. U.S. Fish and Wildl. Serv., FWS/OBS-84/09. Washington, D.C. 134 pp.

Gosselink, J. G. and R. H. Baumann. 1980. Wetland inventories: wetland loss along the United States coast. Z. Geomorph. N.F., Suppl. 34:173–87.

Gosselink, J. G., C. L. Cordes, and J. W. Parsons. 1979. An ecological characterization study of the Chenier Plain coastal ecosystem of Louisiana and Texas. U.S. Fish and Wildl. Serv., FWS/OBS-78/9. Washington, D.C. 302 pp.

Gottschalk, J. S. 1981. A concept of management for Chesapeake Bay. Trans. N. Am. Wildl. and Nat. Resources Conf. 46:311–17.

Gould, H. R. and E. M. Farlan, Jr. 1959. Geologic history of the Chenier Plain, Southwest Louisiana. Trans. Gulf Coast Assoc. Geol. Soc. 9:237–70.

Gunter, G. 1967. Some relationships of estuaries to the fisheries of the Gulf of Mexico. Pp. 621–38 *in* Lauff, G. H. (ed.). Estuaries. Amer. Assoc. for the Advancement of Sci. Publ. No. 83. Washington, D.C.

Hackney, C. T. and A. A. de la Cruz. 1981. Effects of fire on brackish marsh communities: management implications. Wetlands 1:75–86.

Harris, V. T. and R. H. Chabreck. 1958. Some effects of hurricane Audrey on the marsh at Marsh Island, Louisiana. Proc. La. Acad. Sci. 21:47–50.

Harris, V. T. and F. J. Webert. 1962. Nutria feeding activity and its effect on marsh vegetation in southwestern Louisiana. Special Sci. Rep.: Wildl. No. 64. U.S. Fish and Wildl. Serv. Washington, D.C. 51 pp.

Hatton, R. S., R. D. DeLaune, and W. H. Patrick, Jr. 1983. Sedimentation, accretion, and subsidence in marshes of Barataria Basin, Louisiana. Limnol. Oceanogr. 28:494–502.

Hedgpeth, J. W. 1947. The Laguna Madre of Texas. Trans. N. Am. Wildl. Conf. 12:364–80.

Hedgpeth, J. W. and S. Obrebski. 1981. Willapa Bay: a historical perspective and a rationale for research. U.S. Fish and Wildl. Serv., FWS/OBA-81/03. Washington, D.C. 52 pp.

Helm, R. N. 1982. Chronological nesting study of common and purple gallinules in the marshlands and rice fields of southwest Louisiana. M.S. thesis. La. State Univ., Baton Rouge. 114 pp.

Herke, W. H. 1971. Use of natural and semi-impounded Louisiana tidal marshes as nurseries for fish and crustaceans. Ph.D. dissertation. La. State Univ., Baton Rouge. 242 pp.

Hoffman, J. S., D. Keys, and J. G. Titus. 1983. Predicting future sea level rise: methodology, estimates to the year 2100 and research needs. Environmental Protection Agency. Washington, D.C. 121 pp.

Hotchkiss, N. 1967. Underwater and floating-leaved plants of the United States and Canada. Bureau of Sports Fish and Wildl. Resource Publ. 44. 124 pp.

Inman, D. L. and C. E. Nordstrom. 1971. On the tectonic and morphologic classification of coasts. J. Geol. 79:1–21.

Joanen, T. 1969. Nesting ecology of alligators in Louisiana. Proc. Ann. Conf. Southeast. Assoc. Game and Fish Comm. 23:141–51.

Joanen, T., L. McNease, and D. Richard. 1985. The effects of winter flooding on white-tailed deer in southwestern Louisiana. Proc. La. Acad. Sci. 48:109–15.

Jones, C. and F. E. Sylvester. 1978. Open space and programs: results of the 1977 National Urban Recreation Study. Trans. N. Am. Wildl. and Nat. Resources Conf. 43:101–7.

Josselyn, M. 1983. The ecology of San Francisco Bay tidal marshes: a community profile. U.S. Fish and Wildl. Serv., FWS/OBA-83/23. Washington, D.C. 102 pp.

Kinler, Q. J. 1986. Muskrat reproduction and the effects of tidal flooding in Louisiana. M.S. thesis. La. State Univ., Baton Rouge. 90 pp.

Knutson, P. L., J. C. Ford, M. R. Inskeep, and J. Oyler. 1981. National survey of planted salt marshes (vegetative stabilization and wave stress). Wetlands 1:129–57.

Kolb, C. R. and J. R. Van Lopik. 1958. Geology of the Mississippi River deltaic plain—southeastern Louisiana. U.S. Army Eng. Waterways Exp. Stn. Tech. Rep. 2:3–482.

Linscombe, G. and N. Kinler. 1985. Fur harvest distribution in coastal Louisiana. Pp. 187–99 *in* Bryan, C. F., P. J. Zwank, and R. H. Chabreck (eds.). Proc. 4th Coastal Marsh and Estuary Manage. Symp. La. State Univ., Baton Rouge.

Lloyd, F. E. and S. M. Tracy. 1901. The insular flora of Mississippi and Louisiana. Bull. Torr. Bot. Club 28:61–101.

Lowery, G. H., Jr. 1974a. Louisiana birds. La. State Univ. Press, Baton Rouge. 651 pp.

Lowery, G. H., Jr. 1974b. The mammals of Louisiana and adjacent waters. La. State Univ. Press, Baton Rouge. 565 pp.

Lowery, G. H., Jr. and R. J. Newman. 1954. The birds of the Gulf of Mexico. Pp. 519–40 *in*

Galtsoff, P. S. (ed.). Gulf of Mexico Its Origin, Waters, and Marine Life. U.S. Fish and Wildl. Serv. Fishery Bull. 89. Washington, D.C.

Lynch, J. J. 1941. The place of burning in management of the Gulf Coast refuges. J. Wildl. Manage. 5:454–58.

Lynch, J. J. 1968. Values of the South Atlantic and Gulf Coast marshes and estuaries to waterfowl. Pp. 51–63 *in* Newsom, J. D. (ed.). Proc. Marsh and Estuary Manage. Symp., La. State Univ., Baton Rouge.

Lynch, J. J., T. O'Neil and D. W. Lay. 1947. Management significance of damage by geese and muskrats to Gulf Coast marshes. J. Wildl. Manage. 2:50–76.

Lytle, S. A. and B. N. Driskell. 1954. Physical and chemical characteristics of the peats, mucks, and clays of the coastal marsh area of St. Mary Parish, Louisiana. La. Agric. Exp. Sta. Bull. 484. 37 pp.

Macdonald, K. B. 1977. Plant and animal communities of Pacific North American salt marshes. Pp. 167–91 *in* Chapman, V. J. (ed.). Ecosystems of the World. I. West Coastal Ecosystems. Elsevier Scientific Publ., New York.

Malone, R. 1986. A turtle's race against time. Aquanotes 15(2):1–5.

Marmer, H. A. 1954. Tides and sea level in the Gulf of Mexico. Pp. 101–18 *in* Galtsoff, P. S. (ed.). Gulf of Mexico Its Origin, Waters, and Marine Life. U.S. Fish and Wildl. Serv. Fishery Bull. 89. Washington, D.C.

Mason, H. L. 1957. A flora of the marshes of California. Univ. Calif. Press, Berkeley. 878 pp.

Mason, H. L. 1980. Techniques for creating salt marshes along the California coast. Pp. 23–24 *in* Lewis, J. C. and E. W. Bunce (eds.). Rehabilitation and Creation of Selected Coastal Habitats: Proceedings of a Workshop. U.S. Fish and Wildl. Serv., FWS/OBS-80/27. Washington, D.C.

McKenzie, P. M. 1985. Indices of mottled duck abundance and habitat use in agricultural areas of southwestern Louisiana. M.S. thesis. La. State Univ., Baton Rouge. 111 pp.

McNease, L. and T. Joanen. 1978. Distribution and relative abundance of the alligator in Louisiana coastal marshes. Proc. Ann. Conf. Southeast. Assoc. Game and Fish Comm. 32:182–86.

Meade, R. H. 1969. Landward transport of bottom sediments in estuaries of the Atlantic coastal plain. J. Sediment. Petrol. 39:222–34.

Mendelssohn, I. A., K. L. McKee, and M. T. Postek. 1982. Sublethal stresses controlling *Spartina alterniflora* productivity. Pp. 223–42 *in* Gopal, B., R. E. Turner, R. G. Wetzel, and D. F. Wigham (eds.). Wetlands Ecology and Management. Proc. 1st Int. Wetlands Conf., New Delhi.

Morgan, J. P. 1973. Impact of subsidence and erosion on Louisiana coastal marshes and estuaries. Pp. 217–33 *in* Chabreck R. H. (ed.). Proc. 2nd Coastal Marsh and Estuary Manage. Symp., La. State Univ., Baton Rouge.

Morgan, P. H., A. S. Johnson, W. P. Baldwin, and J. L. Landers. 1975. Characteristics and management of tidal impoundments for wildlife in a South Carolina estuary. Proc. Ann. Conf. Southeast. Assoc. Game and Fish Comm. 29:526–39.

Muenscher, W. C. 1964. Aquatic plants of the United States. Cornell Univ. Press, Ithaca, N.Y. 374 pp.

National Ocean Service. 1986a. Tide tables 1987 high and low water predictions East Coast of North and South America. U.S. Dept. of Commerce. Washington, D.C. 289 pp.

National Ocean Service. 1986b. Tide tables 1987 high and low water predictions West Coast of North and South America including the Hawaiian Islands. U.S. Dept. of Commerce. Washington, D.C. 234 pp.

Neely, W. W. 1958. Irreversible drainage — a new factor in waterfowl management. Trans. N. Am. Wildl. Conf. 23:342–48.

Neely, W. W. 1962. Saline soils and brackish waters in management of wildlife, fish, and shrimp. Trans. N. Am. Wildl. and Nat. Resources Conf. 27:321–34.

Neely, W. W. 1968. Planting, disking, mowing, and grazing. Pp. 212–221 *in* Newsom, J. D. (ed.). Proc. Marsh and Estuary Manage. Symp., La. State Univ., Baton Rouge.

Nichols, J. D., L. Viehman, R. H. Chabreck, and B. Fenderson. 1976. Simulations of a commercially harvested alligator population in Louisiana. La. Agr. Exp. Stn. Bull. 691. 59 pp.

Nichols, L. G. 1958. Erosion of canal banks on the Rockefeller Wildlife Refuge. La. Wildl. Life and Fisheries Comm., New Orleans. 11 pp.

Nichols, L. G. 1959. Geology of Rockefeller Wildlife Refuge and Game Preserve. La. Wildl. Life and Fisheries Comm., New Orleans. 159 pp.

Nixon, S. W. 1980. Between coastal marshes and coastal waters—a review of twenty years of speculation and research on the role of salt marshes in estuarine productivity and water chemistry. Pp. 437–525 *in* Hamilton, P. and K. B. McDonald (eds.). Estuarine and Wetland Processes; With Emphasis on Modeling. Plenum Press, New York.

Nixon, S. W. 1982. The ecology of New England high salt marshes: a community profile. U.S. Fish and Wildlife Serv., FWS/OBA-81/55. Washington, D.C. 70 pp.

Nixon, S. W. and C. A. Oviatt. 1973. Ecology of a New England salt marsh. Ecol. Monogr. 43:463–98.

Oberholser, H. C. 1938. The bird life of Louisiana. Dept. of Cons., New Orleans. 834 pp.

Odum, W. E., T. J. Smith III, J. K. Hoover, and C. C. McIvor. 1984. The ecology of tidal freshwater marshes of the United States east coast: a community profile. U.S. Fish and Wildl. Serv., FWS/OBS-83/17. Washington, D.C. 177 pp.

Office of Technology Assessments. 1984. Wetlands: their use and regulation. U.S. Gov. Printing Off., Washington, D.C. 208 pp.

O'Neil, T. 1949. The muskrat in the Louisiana coastal marsh. La. Dept. of Wildl. and Fish., New Orleans. 152 pp.

Palmisano, A. W. 1967. Ecology of *Scirpus olneyi* and *Scirpus robustus* in Louisiana coastal marshes. M.S. thesis. La. State Univ., Baton Rouge. 145 pp.

Palmisano, A. W. 1970. Plant communities-soil relationships in Louisiana coastal marshes. Ph.D. dissertation. La. State Univ. Baton Rouge. 98 pp.

Palmisano, A. W. 1971. The effects of salinity on the germination and growth of plants important to wildlife in the Gulf Coast marshes. Proc. Annu. Conf. Southeast. Assoc. Game and Fish Comm. 25:215–23.

Palmisano, A. W. 1973. Habitat preferences of waterfowl and fur animals in the Northern Gulf Coasts Marshes. Pp. 163–90 *in* Chabreck, R. H. (ed.). Proc. 2nd Coastal Marsh and Estuary Manage. Symp., La. State Univ., Baton Rouge.

Palmisano, A. W. and R. H. Chabreck. 1972. The relationship of plant communities and soils of the Louisiana coastal marshes. Proc. La. Assoc. of Agronomists 13:72–101.

Penfound, W. T. and E. S. Hathaway. 1938. Plant communities in the marshlands of southeastern Louisiana. Ecol. Monogr. 8:1–56.

Penland, S. and R. Boyd. 1982. Assessment of geological and human factors responsible for Louisiana coastal barrier erosion. Pp. 14–38 *in* Boesch, D. F. (ed.). Proc. of the Conf. on Coastal Erosion and Modification in La.: Causes, Consequences, and Options. U.S. Fish and Wildl. Serv., FWS/OBS-82/59. Washington, D.C.

Penland, S., J. Suter, and L. Nakashima. 1986. Protecting our barrier islands. La. Conservationist 38(1):22–25.

Perry, M. C., R. E. Monro, and G. M. Haramis. 1981. Twenty-five year trends in diving duck populations in Chesapeake Bay. Trans. N. Am. Wildl. and Nat. Resources Conf. 46:299–310.

Perry, W. G., Jr., T. Joanen, and L. McNease. 1970. Crawfish-waterfowl, a multiple use concept for impounded marshes. Proc. Ann. Conf. Southeast. Assoc. Game and Fish Comm. 24:506-19.

Pethick, J. 1974. The distribution of salt pans on tidal marshes. J. Biogeogr. 1:57-62.

Phleger, F. B. 1977. Soils of marine marshes. Pp. 69-77 *in* Chapman, V. J. (ed.). Ecosystem of the World. I. Wet Coastal Ecosystems. Elsevier Scientific Publ., New York.

Provost, M. W. 1968. Managing impounded salt marshes for mosquito control and estuarine resources conservation. Pp. 163-71 *in* Newsom, J. D. (ed.). Proc. Marsh and Estuary Manage. Symp., La. State Univ., Baton Rouge.

Redfield, A. C. 1967. The ontogeny of a salt marsh. Pp. 108-14 *in* Lauff, G. H. (ed.). Estuaries. Amer. Assoc. for the Advancement of Sci. Publ. No. 83. Washington, D.C.

Redfield, A. C. 1972. Development of a New England salt marsh. Ecol. Monogr. 42:201-37.

Reimold, R. J. 1976. Grazing on wetland meadows. Pp. 219-25 *in* Wiley, M. (ed.). Estuarine Processes: Uses, Stresses, and Adaptation to the Estuary. Vol. 1. Academic Press, New York.

Reimold, R. J. 1977. Mangals and salt marshes of eastern United States. Pp. 157-66 *in* Chapman, V. J. (ed.). Ecosystems of the World. I. Wet Coastal Ecosystems. Elsevier Scientific Publ. New York.

Reimold, R. J. and M. A. Hardisky. 1978. Non-consumption use values of wetlands. Pp. 558-64 *in* Greeson, P. E., J. R. Clark, and J. E. Clark (eds.). Wetland Functions and Values: the State of Our Understanding. Am. Water Resources Assoc., Minneapolis.

Richards, L. A. 1954. Diagnosis and improvement of saline and alkaline soils. U.S. Dept. of Agri. Handbook 60. 196 pp.

Rogers, B. D. and W. H. Herke. 1985. Estuarine-dependent fish and crustacean movements and weir management. Pp. 201-19 *in* Bryan, C. F., P. J. Zwank, and R. H. Chabreck (eds.). Proc. 4th Coastal Marsh and Estuary Manage. Symp., La. State Univ., Baton Rouge.

Rollings, C. T. and R. L. Warden 1964. Weedkillers and waterfowl. Pp. 593-98 *in* Linduska, J. P. (ed.). Waterfowl Tomorrow. U.S. Fish and Wildl. Serv., Washington, D.C.

Rorabaugh, J. C. and P. J. Zwank. 1983. Habitat suitability index models: mottled duck. U.S. Fish and Wildl. Serv., FWS/OBS-82/10.52. Washington, D.C. 26 pp.

Ross, W. M. and R. H. Chabreck. 1972. Factors affecting the growth and survival of natural and planted stands of *Scirpus olneyi*. Proc. Annu. Conf. Southeast. Assoc. Game and Fish Comm. 26:178-88.

Rote, J. W. 1981. Role of the National Marine Fisheries Service in the protection of freshwater inflow to estuaries. Pp. 18-22 *in* Cross, R. and D. Williams (eds.). Proc. Nat. Symp. on Freshwater Inflow to Estuaries. Vol. 1. U.S. Fish and Wildl. Serv., FWS/OBS-81/04. Washington, D.C.

Russell, R. J. 1942. Flotant. Geographical Review 32:74-98.

Russell, R. J. 1957. Instability of sea level. Am. Scientist 45:414-30.

Russell, R. J. 1967. Origins of estuaries. Pp. *in* Lauff, G. H. (ed.). Estuaries. Publ. No. 83. Am. Assoc. for the Advance. of Sci., Washington, D.C.

St. Amant, L. S. 1959. Louisiana wildlife inventory and management plan. La. Wild Life and Fish. Comm., New Orleans. 329 pp.

Salyer, J. C., II, and F. G. Gillett. 1964. Federal refuges. Pp. 497-508 *in* Linduska, J. P. (ed.). Waterfowl Tomorrow. U.S. Gov. Printing Off., Washington, D.C.

Sanderson, G. C. and F. C. Bellrose. 1969. Wildlife habitat management of wetlands. An. Acad. Brasil. Cienc. (Suplemento) 41:153-204.

Self, C. F., R. H. Chabreck, and T. Joanen. 1974. Food preferences of deer in Louisiana coastal marshes. Proc. Annu. Conf. Southeast. Assoc. Game and Fish Comm. 28:548-56.

Seliskar, D. M. and J. L. Gallagher. 1983. The ecology of tidal marshes of the Pacific Northwest coast: a community profile. U.S. Fish and Wildl. Serv., FWS/OBS-82/32. Washington, D.C. 65 pp.

Seneca, E. D. 1980. Techniques for creating salt marshes along the east coast. Pp. 1–5 *in* Lewis, J. C. and E. W. Bunce (eds.). Rehabilitation and Creation of Selected Coastal Habitats: Proceedings of a Workshop. U.S. Fish and Wildl. Serv., FWS/OBS-80/27. Washington, D.C.

Shaw, S. P. and C. G. Fredine. 1954. Wetlands of the United States. U.S. Fish and Wild. Serv. Circ. 39. Washington, D.C. 67 pp.

Shealy, P. M. and P. J. Zwank. 1981. Activity patterns of a nesting pair of southern bald eagles in southern Louisiana. Pp. 127–29 *in* Odum, R. R. and J. W. Guthrie (eds.). Proc. Nongame and Endangered Wildl. Symp., Ga. Dept. Nat. Res. Tech. Bull. WL5. Athens, Ga.

Smith, H. K. 1977, Habitat development aspects of the dredged material research program. Trans. N. Am. Wildl. and Nat. Resources Conf. 42:93–101.

Smith, K. C. 1969. A technique for capturing white-tailed deer in the delta marsh by use of air-boats and helicopters. Proc. Ann. Conf. Southeast. Assoc. Game and Fish Comm. 23:59–67.

Smith, T. J., III and W. E. Odum. 1981. The effects of grazing by snow geese on coastal salt marshes. Ecology 62:90–106.

Soil Conservation Service. 1984. Prescribed burning for wildlife in the coastal marshes. U.S. Dept. of Agric., Alexandria, La. 2 pp.

Spiller, S. F. and R. H. Chabreck. 1975. Wildlife populations in coastal marshes influenced by weirs. Proc. Ann. Conf. Southeast. Assoc. Game and Fish Comm. 29:518–25.

Sprunt, A., IV. 1968. Values of the South Atlantic and Gulf Coast marshes and estuaries to birds other than waterfowl, Pp. 64–72 *in* Newsom, J. D. (ed.). Proc. Marsh and Estuary Manage. Symp., La. State Univ., Baton Rouge.

Steers, J. A. 1977. Physiography. Pp. 31–60 *in* Chapman, V. J. (ed.). Ecosystems of the World. I. Wet Coastal Ecosystems. Elsevier Scientific Publ., New York.

Stewart, R. E. 1962. Waterfowl populations in the Upper Chesapeake region. U.S. Fish and Wildl. Spec. Sci. Rep. Wildl. No. 65. Washington, D.C. 208 pp.

Stout, J. P. 1984. The ecology of irregularly flooded salt marshes of the northeastern Gulf of Mexico: a community profile. U.S. Fish and Wildl. Serv. Biol. Rep. 85(7.1). 98 pp.

Sverdrup, H. U., M. W. Johnson, and R. H. Fleming. 1942. The oceans, their physics, chemistry, and general biology. Prentice-Hall, New York. 1087 pp.

Sykes, J. E. 1968. Commercial values of estuarine-generated fisheries of the South Atlantic and Gulf of Mexico coasts. Pp. 73–78 *in* Newsom, J. D. (ed.). Proc. Marsh and Estuary Manage. Symp., La. State Univ., Baton Rouge.

Teal, J. M. 1962. Energy flow in the salt marsh ecosystem of Georgia. Ecology 43:614–24.

Teal, J. M. 1986. The ecology of regularly flooded salt marshes of New England: a community profile. U.S. Fish and Wildl. Serv. Biol. Rep. 87(7.4). 61 pp.

Teal, J. and M. Teal. 1969. Life and death of the salt marsh. Ballantine Books, New York. 274 pp.

Templet, P. and K. Meyer-Arendt. 1986. Louisiana wetland loss and sea level rise: a regional management approach to the problem. La. State Univ., Baton Rouge. 24 pp.

Titus, J. G. 1985. How to estimate future sea level rise in particular communities. U.S. Environ. Protection Agency, Washington, D.C. 1 p.

Titus, J. G., M. C. Barth, M. J. Gibbs, J. S. Hoffman, and M. Kennedy. 1984a. An overview of the causes and effects of sea level rise. Pp. 1–56 *in* Barth, M. and J. Titus (eds.). Greenhouse effect and sea level rise: a challenge for this generation. Van Nostrand Reinhold, New York.

Titus, J. G., T. R. Henderson, and J. M. Teal. 1984b. Sea level rise and wetland loss in the United States. Nat. Wetland Newsletter 6(5):3–6.

Turner, R. E., R. Costanza, and W. Scaife. 1982. Canals and wetland erosion rates in coastal

Louisiana. Pp. 73–84 *in* Boesch, D. F. (ed.). Proc. Conf. on Coastal Erosion and Modification in La.: Causes, Consequences, and Options. U.S. Fish and Wildl. Serv., FWS/OBS-82/59. Washington, D.C.

U.S. Army Corps of Engineers. 1976. Levees along the lower Mississippi. U.S.A.C.O.E., Miss. River Comm., Vicksburg, Miss. 4 pp.

U.S. Fish and Wildlife Service. 1977. Coastal marsh productivity—a bibliography. U.S. Fish and Wildl. Serv., FWS/OBA-77/3. Washington, D.C. 300 pp.

Valiela, I. and J. M. Teal. 1979. Inputs, outputs, and interconversions of nitrogen in a salt marsh ecosystem. Pp. 399–414 *in* Jefferies, R. L. and A. J. Davy (eds.). Ecological Processes in Coastal Environments. Blackwell Scientific Publ., Oxford, England.

Valiela, I., S. Vince, and J. M. Teal. 1976. Assimilation of sewerage by wetlands. Pp. 234–53 *in* Wiley, M. (ed.). Estuarine Processes: Uses, Stresses, and Adaptation to the Estuary. Vol. 1. Academic Press, New York.

Waisel, Y. 1972. Biology of halophytes. Academic Press, New York. 395 pp.

Weller, M. W. and C. E. Spatcher. 1965. Role of habitat in the distribution and abundance of marsh birds. Iowa Agric. and Home Econ. Exp. Sta. Spec. Rep. No. 43, Ames. 31 pp.

West, R. C. 1977. Tidal salt-marsh and mangal formations of Middle and South America. Pp. 193–213 *in* Chapman, V. J. (ed.). Ecosystems of the World. I. Wet Coastal Ecosystems. Elsevier Scientific Publ., New York.

Whitlatch, R. B. 1982. The ecology of New England tidal flats: a community profile. U.S. Fish and Wildl. Serv., FWS/OBS-81/01. Washington, D.C. 125 pp.

Whitney, D. M., A. G. Chalmers, E. B. Haines, R. B. Hanson, L. R. Pomeroy, and B. Sherr. 1981. The cycles of nitrogen and phosphorus. Pp. 163–81 *in* Pomeroy, L. R. and R. G. Wiegert (eds.). The Ecology of a Salt Marsh. Springer-Verlag, New York.

Williams, S. O., III and R. H. Chabreck. 1986. Quantity and quality of waterfowl habitat in Louisiana. School of For., Wildl, and Fish. Res. Rep. No. 8, Baton Rouge. 84 pp.

Wilson, C. L. and W. E. Loomis. Botany. Holt, Rinehart, and Winston, New York. 528 pp.

Wilson, K. A. 1968. Fur production on southeastern coastal marshes. Pp. 149–62 *in* Newsom, J. D. (ed.). Proc. Marsh and Estuary Manage. Symp., La. State Univ., Baton Rouge.

Zedler, J. B. 1982. The ecology of southern California coastal salt marshes: a community profile. U.S. Fish and Wildl. Serv., FWS/OBS-81/54. Washington, D.C. 110 pp.

Index

Index

A professor of wildlife management at Louisiana State University since 1972, **Robert Chabreck** received his Ph.D. in botany (1970) and M.S. in wildlife management (1956) from Louisiana State University. For over 30 years he has pursued research on plant and animal management in coastal zones. Chabreck has been employed as a consultant for numerous corporations and government agencies, including the Louisiana Wildlife and Fisheries Commission (1957–67); U.S. Department of Interior, Louisiana Cooperative Wildlife Research Unit (1967–72); and U.S. Department of Interior, National Coastal Ecosystems Team (1975–76). He is active in such professional organizations as The Wildlife Society, the Society of Wetland Scientists, the S.E. Section Wildlife Society, and the Mississippi Flyway Council Technical Section. Chabreck has published over 100 papers dealing with wildlife, wetlands, and land management. He is author of *Common Vascular Plants of the Louisiana Coastal Marshes* and contributes to *Journal of Wildlife Management* and *The American Naturalist*.